The environment
what every business needs to know

Stewart Anthony

First published in 2005 by Middlesex University Press

ISBN 1 904750 09 5

Middlesex University Press Limited
Middlesex University
Queensway Enfield
London EN3 4SA

Designed and typeset by Keyline Consultancy

Printed by St Edmundsbury Press on 100% waste materials

Disclaimers

Information on legislation is provided for general reference, and readers are strongly advised to seek appropriate professional assistance with regard to any aspect of compliance or exposure.

Legislation is correct, to the best of our knowledge, as of December 2004 and is generally applicable to England and Wales; legislation for Scotland and Northern Ireland may differ.

Websites and sources of reference are correct as at December 2004; the inclusion of any organisation, body or company is not to be taken as endorsement of either the organisation or its services; the omission of any organisation is no reflection on that organisation. The author and publishers would be pleased to hear of any additional websites that readers have found useful.

Acknowledgements

This book has been possible only with the help and advice of a number of people. I am particularly indebted to the present staff of the Centre for Environment and Safety Management for Business (CESMB) for their comments on different chapters: Leah Corr who also discussed and tested the initial idea; Ankit Kapasi who also developed several of the practical tasks and contributed many contacts; and Anuj Saush, Juan Velazquez and Susanne Hayward.

Outside CESMB I am grateful to Crispin Webber of Thames Energy Services for his valuable comments on Chapter 5. I should also thank the staff at the North London Chamber of Commerce who, over many years, have stressed the importance of business benefits as part of environmental improvement. Thanks also go to the very many small, medium and large businesses we have worked with who never cease to impress us with their ingenuity, enthusiasm and commitment to integrating environmental improvements into their businesses.

Finally, my gratitude also goes to my wife, Anne, for tolerating many evenings as a 'computer widow' and my children Rebecca, Simon and Matthew for their often helpful and sometimes quirky comments on parts of the book and its overall progress.

Stewart Anthony, December 2004.

Foreword

For many owners and managers in business, the term 'environment' is often viewed as a niggling issue that occasionally veers into their radar – but mostly is difficult to get a grasp of and to translate into something which is meaningful and practical for their business.

For small and medium-sized enterprises (SMEs), the environment is often seen as threat, opportunity, reality, conjecture, imminent threat or latent possibility. How valuable then is this handy overview, which draws the threads together and provides a comprehensive outline of the key environment business issues. It provides a summary of the environmental background for businesses, a balanced overview of the management strategies in relevant environmental areas to businesses and the tactical opportunities offered to organisations to take pre-emptive actions.

Environmental opportunities are driven by a growing structure of regulations, taxes and increasingly complex fiscal instruments. As recently as five years ago, many of these never existed; now they are a key determinant of commercial success – even survival. The implications of each of these policy developments will vary, depending on the nature of your particular organisation, but some or all of these policies will impact on you now, and are likely to have more impact in the future.

In business sector after business sector, the ink is barely dry on relevant regulations, supply chain agreements, insurance details, good practice recommendations and a host of other environmentally inspired directives before the need for innovative thinking, and cost reductions to mitigate the impact of these trends, are required.

This publication is designed to provide a helicopter vision of the inter-relationship between those seemingly disparate elements which comprise 'environmental opportunities'. Absorbing the contents will underline that connectivity – and offer a spur to action, in an area which many believe will form the basis of the next industrial revolution. Each chapter is set out in a similar format, with business-related information and ideas, suggested actions and further information. It is user-friendly and based on over ten years' experience of working with businesses of all sizes.

Peter Jones
Director – External Relations
Biffa Waste Services Ltd

About the author

Stewart Anthony has spent over 30 years working in various aspects of environmental management, education and training. For several years he worked at environmental centres in the Peak District National Park and then in north London. In both centres he was responsible for developing a wide range of ecological and environmental programmes for professional staff, teachers, school groups and the general public.

In the early 1990s he started working with businesses, helping them address environmental issues and gain business benefits from so doing. In 1992 he was given the chance to extend this work by establishing the Centre for Environment and Safety Management for Business (CESMB) at Middlesex University. The Centre has grown and developed steadily over the past 10 years and is now well recognised by many organisations in North London.

Stewart works both as a consultant and a trainer, an adviser and supporter of the many small businesses and business support organisations who want or need CESMB services. His environmental and business expertise is now allied with Health and Safety qualifications and experience, and he has spoken at several national and international conferences and worked in South Africa, India and in Europe.

This book pulls together much of the knowledge, understanding and ideas that Stewart has acquired during this work with businesses, but he recognises that the very nature of the subject matter means that the content will regularly require updates as developments take place.

He is happy to hear from any readers with constructive comments about the book and its content, or any businesses or other organisations that might wish to contact him professionally. Please contact him at:

Stewart55anthony@hotmail.com

Contents

Part 1: The background

Introduction

> ### Case study
>
> North London Chamber of Commerce has worked closely over many years with CESMB at Middlesex University to help its members appreciate environmental issues. It runs a 'Business Environment Network' in the area and has a green section in its magazines. This all helps to highlight the fact that the environment is an important business issue and that expert help is readily available.

1.1 Overview

What has the environment got to do with small businesses? Many would suggest 'not much' – and several spurious arguments have been put forward to defend that view. Either the business operates in the service sector (and staff believe that the environment does not affect what they do) or they say that their business does not actually cause any pollution, create significant waste or carry out other activities which impact upon the environment. Even if the small business *does* affect the environment, many people feel the extent of that impact is so small as to be insignificant.

The most 'ostrich-like' argument says that, even if the business *does* have an effect on the environment, there are plenty of other businesses which are much worse, causing pollution, dumping large amounts of waste and even operating in a rather unsafe way. Typical of the comments received when discussing environmental issues with small businesses are:

> 'Well, my business would like to take more care about the environment but quite frankly it will cost too much, and we operate in a very competitive arena and just cannot afford to make these changes because it will put us out of business.'

> 'Yes, we do care about the environment and we have made some changes, such as recycling paper and cutting our energy use, but we are competing against products from overseas where their labour costs are much less and they are not under the same pressures for environmental improvement. These overseas firms are the people who should really be making improvements.'

These are just two of the opinions and views expressed by owners and managers of small businesses to explain why they consider the environment as something which they should not have to worry about; but there is another side to the coin, as the following views indicate:

> '60% of our business is with X and they are asking us to demonstrate how we are applying an environmental policy, so this is clearly the way things are going, so let's get serious about environmental improvements.'

> 'The environment is important and we want to try to do what we can to help.'

> 'We are prepared to do our bit for the environment if everybody else does their bit.'

With opinions varying from one extreme to the other, and with a variety of other views somewhere between, it is perhaps appropriate to offer some direction, help and encouragement to small businesses to assist them making environmental improvements.

That is precisely the aim of this book: to be a handy desktop manual which provides information, help, advice and guidance to help small and medium-sized businesses make changes which will benefit them as well as the environment. Managers within larger businesses will also find the content helpful and providing food for thought, even though many of the wider issues would be addressed by specialists within the company.

So why should small businesses be concerned with the environment? Let's respond to some of the most common comments:

■ *'We operate in the service sector and really we do not damage the environment, and the environment does not really affect us.'*

Every single business has an effect on the environment, maybe not very large, but in several important ways. Every business consumes energy, and this in turn contributes to global climate change. Every business produces waste which, in the UK, is carried to landfill sites for dumping. Landfill sites are rapidly disappearing and the cost of waste disposal is increasing – and some waste is a serious pollutant. On a local scale, many businesses contribute to transport congestion on roads, either through the services they provide, deliveries they receive or their staff travelling to and from work. This is not to suggest that this transport should not take place, but consideration should be given as to how it can be done with less environmental impact.

■ *'We are only a small business, so the amount of environmental damage we can cause is so small that it does not justify making any changes.'*

Strictly speaking, that is true: most businesses, and each person, have an impact that *individually* has no measurable effect on the environment. However, we live in a society, and businesses are part of a community; one of the tenets of modern societies and communities is that the individuals within it should practise behaviours which are to the benefit of that group or, at least, not to the detriment of that group. Many of the improvements and changes in individual and organisational practices are started by a few individuals doing things differently; this can then 'snowball' until a significant change is produced. It is worth remembering the quote from the 18th-century political theorist, Edmund Burke: 'No man made a greater mistake than he who did nothing because he could do so little.'

■ *'We cannot afford to make environmental improvements: it will cost money and make us uncompetitive.'*

This is, in almost all cases, simply incorrect.   All the evidence from businesses that have improved their environmental performance is that they make significant commercial gains.   Many improvements can be made at no cost: at its simplest, organisations can improve their environmental and business performance just by tackling their energy consumption.   Studies have shown that most businesses can save about 10% of their energy consumption with no investment, simply by changing practices and adjusting heating and lighting controls.   In the UK, due to the increasingly expensive cost of waste disposal, most businesses will also save considerable sums of money by implementing an effective waste-minimisation strategy.

■ *'We will make changes if the law demands it, but we see no reason why we should go beyond the legal requirements.'*

Research suggests that most businesses in the UK fall into this category – that is, that they will comply with the legislation, but go no further. However, this shows a somewhat short-sighted approach to some of the changes which are occurring.   One of the features of environmental legislation is that it is continually changing and developing: new laws are introduced and existing laws are tightened.   The reason for this is that new products and materials are being produced and legislation needs to be modified or developed to take account of these materials or processes.   In addition, as research extends we become increasingly aware of the environmental and health damage that is occurring; consequently, laws are changed to reflect this new knowledge.   This should also cause businesses to consider their investment strategy in new equipment.   We are aware of several instances in which companies have invested in new equipment which satisfied the legal requirements at the time of purchase.   However, after a few years the legislation tightens and the equipment fails to meet the new legal standards; further investment in improved equipment or modification of the existing equipment is needed.

Although performing only to the minimum legal standard is, of course, acceptable, it can in fact be more expensive for the company – and will not reflect a long-term strategy to overall improvements.

■ *'We will make changes if it is financially beneficial and the payback period is not too long.'*

It is perfectly reasonable to expect businesses to want to make improvements in their environmental performance which also have financial benefits to the business.   However, the criteria that businesses employ in making their cost/benefit analysis will determine the extent to which they are more, or less, likely to purchase equipment with improved environmental specifications.   At one extreme are organisations which purchase equipment or materials simply on the basis of the capital cost, and pay little heed to the running and maintenance costs.   Some companies we have worked with have indicated that their senior management ruled that there should be a maximum one-year payback period, which effectively rules out most purchases which exceed the lowest price.   More realistic timescales, as employed by other businesses, suggest payback periods of about three years, and also consider the nature of the purchase. Consideration needs to be given not only to the *running and maintenance* costs of the alternative types of equipment but, increasingly, also to the *disposal* costs.   Chapter 8, on purchasing and supply issues, provides guidelines on the selection of materials and equip..ient with environmental criteria.

■   *'If we are pushed too far, this company will move its operation overseas where the constraints are less.'*

Increasingly, products and materials are sourced from overseas because the production costs are lower than in the UK and because there is also a pattern of less extensive and less rigorous environmental legislation. One of the important features that is demanded by many environmental organisations is the need for a globally uniform pattern of environmental legislation.   The reason for this is that environmental protection should be considered as a global objective – but with local responsibilities.   It makes little sense, for example, if western Europe cleans its environment and operates to high environmental standards, while importing goods from Africa or Asia which have been produced in a way damaging to the environment.   Similarly, any protection afforded to the Mediterranean by southern European countries could easily be undone if North African countries perform to low environmental standards and pollute the sea. This, of course, applies to any body of water: protection will only be effective if *all* bordering territories perform to similar environmental standards.

It should also be recognised that purchasers, in general, are increasingly interested in the quality of products and services, and environmental criteria should be considered as an aspect of quality.   There is an argument that locally produced goods of higher quality should be marketed with these qualities emphasised.

■   *'We don't have the spare staff to undertake some of the necessary steps.'*

In the UK, throughout the 1980s and subsequently, there has been a drive towards increased efficiency.   This has invariably resulted in staff reduction, because most organisations identified that staff costs were their most significant expenditure.   This has resulted in many organisations having little flexibility with regard to their internal staffing when they need to make changes to processes and operations. For most organisations, there is a perception that environmental improvements require significant staff time and that the environment is not of sufficient immediate priority to justify this; many, therefore, buy in external advice and help in order to make the changes. The problem with this approach is that frequently the changes are not internalised and may not be long term.   The other point to consider is that many environmental improvements do not require *additional* staff time – rather they require *different* staff performance and behaviours; while this may take additional time to introduce, the staffing requirement should be no greater once the changes are established.

■   *'The environmental problems are global and need to be sorted out by politicians; we will do our part but they need to lead.'*

Many of the major environmental problems are indeed global and although nations and their politicians do have a role to play, the ultimate solution to the problems lies with people and the organisations in which they live and work. International politicians need to make agreements to try to solve problems but the reality will be that any agreements will result in national legislation. So businesses which recognise that there are global problems need to examine the likely national consequences of global actions, and take steps to establish their business with processes and technologies which can respond positively and proactively to the developments that are likely to occur.

1.2 Environmental issues

There have been many publications, research reports and documents which set out the extent and variety of issues which are affecting the global environment.   Perhaps the earliest publication which drew attention to some of the problems was Rachel Carson's *Silent Spring* (Penguin Books Ltd, 2000, ISBN 0141184949). Although this book concentrated on the impact of pesticides on the natural world, the evidence of impacts of a wider range of human activity on the climate, freshwater and the oceans and the land has been mounting.

The fact that environmental problems are global in context is now well understood and has stimulated two major United Nations conferences: at Rio de Janiero, in 1992, and Johannesburg, in 2002. These were preceded by the United Nations Environment Programme listing, in 1989, what it saw as its 'top ten' global environmental issues. These are shown overleaf.

- Population

- Resource exploitation

- Greenhouse gases and global warming

- Stratospheric ozone and ultra-violet (UV) radiation

- Acid rain

- Deforestation, desertification and soil degradation

- Water resources

- Biological diversity

- Hazardous waste

- Environmental impact of new technologies and materials.

These issues demonstrate two features: they vary from time to time, and they are of different importance in different areas of the planet.

The extent to which these issues vary from time to time is well illustrated by the way in which acid rain has risen up, and then fallen down, the environmental agenda.   The most straightforward explanation of acid rain is that it is a weak sulphuric acid, produced when sulphur dioxide (produced primarily from the burning of coal) mixes with rain in the high atmosphere, before falling to ground.   Consequently, the soil is acidified and this results in the release of aluminium, which poisons plants, notably trees, and leads to the acidification of lakes; this in turn leads to the death of plants and the fish.   In northern Europe and North America in the 1970s, acid rain was a significant problem: frequent television and media coverage of dead and dying fish in Scandinavian lakes, and dying forests in Germany, illustrated the extent and severity of the issue.

In the 1980s, however, global climate change and ozone depletion became more significant and attracted increasing media attention.   This was exemplified, in the UK in the late 1990s, by several summers and winters which were drier and warmer than average and, at the turn of the century, by several large-scale flooding events which were attributed to global climate change. In reality, both land and river management contributed to the problems.

Despite the increased prominence given to global climate change, it does not mean that acid rain is not now a significant issue – indeed, in parts of Scotland and southern Canada there is still significant forest damage caused by acid rain. The global issues identified above vary in importance from one part of the world to another: soil degradation is a serious problem in parts of South America and South East Asia and, indeed, also a problem in many urban industrial areas in Europe, where soil contamination and pollution are being recognised as serious problems which can arise during attempts to redevelop urban 'brownfield' sites.

1.3 The environment in the UK

Within the UK, the environmental issues reflect several of these global problems. Issues of paramount importance are waste, energy consumption, pollution of land and water and the loss of habitats and consequent loss of plant and animal species. Indeed, in spring 2002, the Government announced that its two major environmental concerns were waste and energy consumption. In the case of the UK there are very good reasons why these should be of concern.

1.3.1 Waste and waste disposal

Waste and waste disposal in the UK is a major problem. About 80% of the waste we produce goes to landfill sites; these are rapidly being used up and, because of previous pollution incidents and problems, controls placed on the use of landfill sites are getting tighter. In 1996, the UK Government introduced the Landfill Tax, which requires payments to be made by businesses for all waste sent to landfill. This tax has been increasing year by year and some businesses are now beginning to take serious action to reduce their waste and use of landfill sites. Local authorities also have targets for waste reduction which, in turn, rely on householders to separate their wastes into different types for recycling.

Apart from the decreasing number of landfill sites, there are also environmental imperatives for reducing waste going to landfill. Firstly, much of that waste is organic and can be composted – indeed, many local authorities now sell this compost to the public; this should reduce the amount of peat used in gardens which, in turn, will benefit the plants and animals and the landscapes of peat lands. Secondly, as the materials in landfill sites decompose they give off various gases – notably methane, which is sometimes collected and used as fuel (to replace oil, coal or natural gas) but in most cases escapes into the atmosphere, where it contributes significantly to global warming. The third main reason is that there is a risk of leakage of liquid pollutant from some, notably older, landfill sites; this risk will continue for many decades.

1.3.2 Energy consumption

The other major Government concern about the environment is energy consumption. The UK is a signatory to the Kyoto Protocol, which requires us, by 2010, to reduce CO_2 emissions by 12% (from the 1990 levels). Even if we reach this target, the pressure to reduce CO_2 emissions from burning fossil fuels will continue; the challenge will thus be to continue what we are doing but to do it in a more energy-efficient way and with non-fossil fuel sources. It is not the place of this manual to argue the case about global climate change and the degree to which it is being influenced by man-made activities: the fact that the climate in the UK and elsewhere in the world is changing is becoming increasingly clear. Predicting the ways the climate will change in the next few decades is as difficult as forecasting next month's weather in any part of the UK. The Government is trying to follow the precautionary principle by taking steps to reduce the causes of the problem where it can, so that the consequences of climate change are less damaging and less costly.

The environment within the UK has also been significantly damaged through the loss of habitats and their associated plants and animals. The intensification of farming in the last 50 years, the growth of urban developments and the building and use of motorways throughout the country has marginalised natural habitats. 95% of natural wildflower meadows have been lost, woodland cover is less than 10% of our land surface, but only about 1% can be described as native or ancient. Many thousands of miles of hedgerow have been removed and many rivers have been canalised, dredged and sculpted to maximise water flows. Recent reports of the decline of songbird species on farmland indicate the continued pressure which our wildlife is under. Modern farming methods and the use of pesticides and herbicides has sometimes left the urban areas as a better refuge for wildlife than the countryside.

Pollution is probably one area where the UK has a better record now than it did about 50 years ago. Air quality is better (though in some weather conditions, the extent of nitrous oxides and sulphur oxides creates a serious photochemical smog) and water quality is better in most areas, though spillages and uncontrolled discharges from industrial sites and farms can blight some rivers. The redevelopment of urban land, notably for housing, is showing the considerable extent of land contamination which has occurred and which is difficult to remediate – that is, to clean and return to normal use. However, many of the chemicals now in use in the UK are very complex and sometimes very potent and far-reaching in their effects. So, while pollution issues in the UK may be better than for many decades, we should not be complacent.

The environment is important to all of us: it affects our health, both mental and physical; it provides us with opportunities for sport, recreation, and leisure; it offers potential and actual indicators of environmental health; and it provides aesthetic values for our pleasure. While we all have a part to play in protecting and improving the quality of our environment, there is an obvious requirement (and one which will be persuaded, encouraged or forced) on the business community to perform to better environmental standards.

1.4 Business and the environment

Business has a considerable role to play in helping to protect and improve the environment. This is a view of most national governments and also many national and international environmental organisations. The view of many businesses is that they are prepared to play their part, but that others have their role as well.

There is a sound rationale for this:

- Businesses are an identifiable community and therefore able to be targeted in the application of taxes and legislation.

- Businesses themselves do not have a vote, but their staff do. However, there is no obvious link between how people vote and what is in the best interests of their employer.

- Businesses manufacture or provide services which have a direct impact on the environment and they can be identified and controlled in terms of their environmental impacts.

In addition to these arguments, it is also becoming obvious that good environmental performance leads to good business performance. There is sound evidence that good environmental management in a business has benefits for the 'financial bottom line' – either through not having to pay penalties or fines, a reduction of taxes or investment in more efficient technologies. There is also a link between environmental performance and social issues: generally, staff are happier working for an organisation which takes the environment seriously in the way it works. Businesses which take care of the area around their premises can benefit significantly.

As an example of this, some industrial estates in North London, several years ago, were untidy, littered and generally run-down. There were several instances of *owners* of new businesses wanting to move to an estate, but backing off when they saw the conditions, and other instances where potential *customers* were put off when they visited.

UK businesses are directly responsible for some significant impact on the environment: they consume over 50% of the energy used, and produce about 70% of the total waste generated in the UK (2002 data). The levels of pollutant gases produced and road miles travelled each year are too large to compute but, clearly, the overall impact is very significant.

Not only do businesses have this direct impact on the environment, but also they influence the people and organisations that work with and for them. Significant purchasers of equipment and materials from other businesses can influence the environmental performance of their supply chain.

However, to say businesses have certain impacts on the environment like this is rather generalised; some business sectors may have more impact than others. Clearly, the furniture sector (for example) has a direct effect on woodlands and forests in this country and overseas; the printing sector influences forests; the food sector can influence the type of, and approach to, farming by purchasing food grown in a particular way; and the tourism sector can influence the management of large areas of the countryside and the urban environments.

The environment is, therefore, a topic which should concern every organisation in the UK. There is a direct relationship between each business and the quality of the environment, although clearly some businesses have a greater impact than others, either due to their size or their operation.

Understanding how your business relates to the environment is a first step; actually making improvements is the next step. Involving all your staff is also a key action in order to maximise the improvements. Selecting the improvement steps, and how your business goes about them, will result in savings for your business.

1.5 About this book

This book is *not* meant to be read from cover to cover. It is designed to be a handy manual for quick and easy reference to information relating to different environmental issues; see how they currently (and may in the future) affect the organisation; identify where businesses can go to find out more about the particular issue; and the general and specific help and advice that is available.

Each chapter contains:

- **The background to each environmental issue**
- **Information about the issue** and how it relates to businesses, especially SMEs
- **What businesses need to do** in order to address the issue: this will include case studies, suggested strategies, important actions (including checklists and audits) and potential difficulties and benefits
- **Further sources of help and information**, a list of organisations, websites, and contacts which can help your business.

All of the forms and checklists within the various chapters are reproduced in Chapter 14: Appendix.

1.6 Sources of information

These are national/international organisations covering general environmental topics.

Name   **Information and Internet address**

Business in the Environment

Networking tool for businesses. Look at the website of *Business in the Community* and click on 'environment'.
www.bitc.org.uk

Centre for Alternative Technology

Ideas and demonstrations of environmental technology and lifestyles.
www.cat.org.uk

CESMB   The Centre for Environment and Safety Management for Business, at Middlesex University. Advice on current and forthcoming environmental legislation and compliance.
www.mdx.ac.uk/www/cesmb

DEFRA   UK Government site with wide range of information.
www.defra.gov.uk

DTI   UK Government site with information and sources of grant support.
www.dti.gov.uk

Environment Agency   Excellent site with loads of information and contacts.
www.environment-agency.gov.uk

Envirowise   For practical advice and help on environmental matters – usually free to small business.
www.envirowise.gov.uk

Environment Data Interactive Exchange

Useful and up-to-date regular environmental news.
www.edie.net

Environmental Services Association

Represents the waste management sector.
www.esauk.org

European Environment Agency

Gateway to environmental information.
www.eea.eu.int

Friends of the Earth   Information and ideas.
www.foe.co.uk

Green Book   Information, articles, comments and
discussion.
www.biggreenbook.com

Greenpeace   Global issues and campaigns.
www.greenpeace.org

HMSO   This UK Government website includes the
full text of all legislation enacted by
Parliament. It provides information about
current legislation. Additionally, all new
legislation is immediately (within 24 hours)
available on the website.
www.legislation.hmso.gov.uk/legislation/uk.htm

Society for the Environment (SocEnv)

This organisation consists of professional
bodies and learned societies, and aims to lead
on the development and regulation of
environmental practitioners; with their
newly-granted Royal Charter, they are able to
award the status of Chartered
Environmentalist (CEnv)
www.socenv.org.uk

2

Environmental legislation

Case study

A company in Dorset was fined £8,000 in 2004 because it claimed it did not realise that it had a legal requirement to register for the amount of packaging it was producing. The Environment Agency had written to the company wanting details of its business and the packaging it handled.

Ignorance of the law, in this area as in all other areas, is no defence. Packaging regulations have been around since 1998, and thus a company's legal obligations have been well publicised to all businesses.

2.1 Overview

Environmental legislation has been around a long time. Some of the earliest legislation dates back to the end of the 19th century when the Alkali Inspectorate was set up by the UK Government, in order to control the level of polluting gases and liquids which emanated from the Victorian factories.

Much environmental legislation grew piecemeal until the 1970s when the UK entered the European Community and our environmental legislation was pulled together and organised in a much more holistic way and at a level of detail which was parallel with other countries in the EC.

Most environmental legislation tends to be driven by actual or potential problems with human health. Thus the Alkali Inspectorate was set up in response to the pollution of air and water and consequent disease with the workers living in the affected areas. In the 1950s, the smogs in London which caused the deaths of many people resulted in controls on smoke from chimneys and, in the 1960s, the controls on DDT as a pesticide were introduced because of the impact on birds of prey and concerns about how this might affect humans.

The problem with much of this environmental legislation is that it is retrospective: the law is only enforced when damage is shown to have occurred. The difficulty with the environment is that, when damage does occur, it can take a long time to recover – regardless of what the law says.

2.1.1 Polluter pays

Many environmental organisations have advocated a different approach, one which applies the 'polluter pays' principle. In 1996 it could be argued that the UK Government made its first attempt to apply this approach by setting up a waste disposal system and bringing in the **Landfill Tax**. Essentially, this legislation sets a tax on the amount of waste which a company produces: the more waste, the more taxes. In addition they also established the Landfill Tax Credit Scheme, whereby companies could claim back a large part of the tax in return for paying it towards environmental improvement schemes – though this was effectively disbanded in the 2003 budget.

The second 'polluter pays' legislation was the **Climate Change Levy**, a tax on the amount of gas or electricity a business uses. Both these taxes operate proactively and may indicate the direction in which future environmental legislation will be framed.

2.1.2 The impact of Europe

All the environmental legislation in the UK is guided by European law: the extent of the legislation, the subjects that are addressed and the level of detail are being designed to be contiguous throughout Europe. Furthermore, this legislation is continually changing and developing. One of the most recent pieces of legislation is the **WEEE Directive** (Waste Electrical and Electronic Equipment). This was introduced in 2002 in response to the vast quantity and wide variety of electrical equipment being dumped; much of this equipment contains heavy and precious metals, circuits and batteries (which are reusable) and plastic and other metals (which can be recycled).

Some laws change the level of permitted activity, because as we learn more about the health and environmental impacts of particular chemicals and other substances we need to tighten the law to afford the proper protection to the public.

Environmental legislation in the UK is also being exerted in a firmer way. The **Environmental Protection Act 1990** allows for criminal prosecutions to be made for breaches of some aspects of that law.

2.1.3 International input

There is another level of environmental legislation: the international laws (conventions) made through the United Nations or its Councils. These international agreements focus on the environmental impacts on the atmosphere, the oceans and seas, wildlife and habitats and heritage as well as civil liability. But whereas these conventions are directed at controlling performance of individual nations, their governments in turn enact laws which require improved performance from organisations.

Hence the current Convention on Climate Change (the Kyoto Protocol) sets targets for reducing CO_2 emissions for the UK; the most effective way that this can be achieved is by requiring organisations to reduce their energy consumption, hence the recent Climate Change Levy.

2.2 Information about environmental legislation

For updated guidance on environmental legislation, we suggest you refer to NetRegs, a website established under the auspices of the Environment Agency. Contact information is provided at the end of this chapter.

There are less than a dozen major pieces of environmental legislation which are of concern to businesses. For ease of explanation they are set out in terms of the aspects of the environment that they try to protect. There is, however, one important piece of legislation which covers several aspects of the environment and it is worth setting out first.

2.2.1 Environmental Protection Act 1990

The Environmental Protection Act (EPA) 1990 introduced a system of Integrated Pollution Control (IPC) arising from industrial processes.

Objectives of IPC

There are two objectives:

- To prevent or minimise the release of prescribed substances and to render harmless any such substances which are released.

- To develop an approach to pollution control of discharges from industrial processes to land, water or air in the context of the effect on the environment as a whole.

IPC is managed by the Environment Agency and controls the more polluting processes; it aims to prevent or minimise pollution of any environmental medium.

The control of releases to the atmosphere from less-polluting processes is the responsibility of local authorities.

In short, any organisation which is carrying out a 'scheduled process', (this is, in essence, a process resulting in high levels of pollution of the air or water) requires authorisation from the Environment Agency. That authorisation will require an assessment of the emissions to all three environments – land, water or air – in order to comply with IPC.

In 1996, a piece of legislation was introduced which tries to address the issues of pollution before they cause damage. **Integrated Pollution Prevention and Control (IPPC)** aims to bring those industrial processes with the greatest pollution potential under a harmonised system of integrated control. This approach requires the use of a technique known as Best Available Technology Not Entailing Excessive Cost (BATNEEC), which aims to provide a high level of protection for the environment as a whole.

Significant new areas are included, notably:

- Consumption of raw materials and water
- Energy efficiency
- Regulations on heat, noise, and vibration
- Requirements for waste minimisation, recycling and recovery.

Also, additional processes currently not falling under IPC are expected to fall within the new regulations, involving up to 2,000 additional company sites.

2.2.2 The waste legislation

The disposal of waste is a major concern in the UK. Prior to 1990, the disposal of waste was controlled in a very haphazard way. It was also agreed, internationally, that each country needed to be responsible for the management of its waste within its own boundaries.

The **Environmental Protection Act 1990 (Part II)** provided a clear framework for the management and disposal of wastes. This legislation applies specifically to businesses and other organisations; it does not apply to domestic households.

The disposal of waste is controlled by three main authorities:

- The **Environment Agency** is responsible for the regulatory functions including the administration, supervision and enforcement of licensed activities
- The **Waste Collection Authority** will arrange for the collection of commercial/industrial waste on request
- The **Waste Disposal Authority** is responsible for licensing the privatised waste disposal companies.

The legislation introduced the concept of the **Duty of Care** which applies to anyone who produces, imports, carries, keeps, treats or disposes of controlled waste. A business, therefore, needs to record accurately what waste it produces and to arrange for a properly licensed carrier to dispose of the waste. This carrier will in turn be responsible for taking the waste to a properly licensed disposal site.

The Duty of Care in this legislation relates to the responsibility of *all* parties in the different stages of waste disposal to take responsibility for ensuring that waste that passes through their control is properly disposed. This then extends to the concept of reasonable care to ensure that acts or omissions which can be reasonably foreseen as likely to injure a 'neighbour' must be taken.

The Duty of Care

This concept was created under the **Environmental Protection Act 1990, Section 34 (5).** All businesses produce waste, therefore the Duty of Care applies to you. Section 34(1) of the same Act imposes a Duty of Care on any person who imports, produces, carries, keeps, treats or disposes of controlled waste or, as a broker, has control of such waste.

The duty requires such persons to ensure that there is no unauthorised or harmful deposit, treatment or disposal of the waste, to prevent the escape of the waste from their control or that of any other person. The legislation is also meant to ensure that the transfer of the waste is only to an authorised person or to a person for authorised transport purposes, and that a written description of the waste is also transferred.

As a waste producer, your business needs to follow these simple steps to meet the Duty of Care legislation requirements:

■ **Step 1: Keep and store your waste securely.** Keep it in a suitable container. If you put loose waste in a skip or any other container, cover it

■ **Step 2: Check whether your waste carrier has the authority** to take the waste. Legally, the person who takes your waste must be authorised to do so

■ **Step 3: You must describe your waste in writing.** You must fill in and sign a transfer note for it, and keep a copy of the transfer note. You can describe the waste on the transfer note.

2.2.3 The Landfill Directive

The **Landfill (England and Wales) Regulations 2002** came into force on 15 June 2002. These new regulations implement the **Landfill Directive (Council Directive 1999/31/EC)**, which aims to prevent, or to reduce as far as possible, the negative environmental effects of landfill. The regulations had a major impact on waste regulation and industry in the UK.

Existing landfills must demonstrate that they comply with the directive if they wish to continue to operate. The ability to comply will be reviewed through a conditioning plan form that must have been submitted to the Environment Agency in 2002, which reclassified the site as inert, hazardous or non-hazardous. The directive also bans liquids and certain materials from landfill and tightens site monitoring and engineering standards.

Though this directive does not impose any *direct* financial burden on the businesses, the costs of following this legislation will, eventually, come down to businesses.

2.2.4 Packaging waste

The **Producer Responsibility Obligations (Packaging Waste) Regulations 1997** sets targets for the recycling and recovery of packaging waste. This legislation sets targets for businesses over a certain size to recover or recycle packaging waste. Many businesses, however, have entered into agreements with packaging waste management companies, who take over the administrative and financial issues associated with the disposal of packaging waste.

If your company has a turnover in excess of £5 million per year *and* is responsible for handling more than 50 tonnes of packaging each year, then your business is affected by this packaging legislation.

EU member states and the European Parliament have reached agreement on a proposal to amend the legislation on packaging and packaging waste, following discussions in early December. The draft law sets new higher targets for the recovery and recycling of packaging, but also attempts to clarify the definition of what is (and is not) packaging waste.

The agreement still has to be formally ratified by the UK Parliament and the Council of Ministers, but it is expected that it will enter into force early in 2004 and will have to be implemented in national law in the second half of 2005.

2.2.5 Legislation protecting different environmental elements

Air

Until recently, most concern about air quality was directed at smoke; now, however, increasing concern is being caused by even small amounts of chemicals and particulate matter, many of which are being shown to be related to respiratory diseases, cancers and other problems.

Air pollution has several impacts on the environment:

- Harmful gases or particles may be inhaled by people or animals or may attack skin, causing ill health or death
- Gases may damage leaves and shoots of plants, reducing amenity and the yields of crops and trees
- Particles or substances which settle onto soil or vegetation may cause damage or contaminate human or animal food
- Air pollution can screen out sunlight, corrode structures and cause a nuisance in many ways, especially through smells and the settlement of airborne dust.

There were four previous pieces of legislation which are now subsumed within the **Clean Air Act 1993**:

- The **Public Health (Smoke Abatement) Act 1926** attempted to control certain categories of industrial smoke. Domestic smoke was prohibited only if it was a 'nuisance'

- The **Clean Air Acts of 1956** and **1968** provided a comprehensive control mechanism for the protection of the environment from smoke, dust and fumes. The law introduced concepts such as smoke control areas and the complete prohibition of 'dark smoke' from chimneys

- The **Air Quality Standards Regulations 1989** introduced mandatory air quality standards. This included ensuring that levels of sulphur dioxide (SO_2), nitrogen dioxide (NO_2), lead (Pb) and smoke do not rise above EU limits.

The Clean Air Act 1993 controls smoke, dust and grit from all fires and furnaces. Its main characteristics are:

- Emission of 'dark smoke' is prohibited from the chimney of any building

- The emission of dark smoke from premises must be controlled, even if there is no chimney

- Measures must be taken to prevent smoke, dust, grit, and fumes being emitted from furnaces

- Permission must be obtained before a furnace is installed

- Grit and dust arrestment equipment must be fitted to furnaces

- Application for chimney height must be approved

- Local authorities have designated 'smoke control areas'. This means that occupiers of any premises (within those designated areas) which allow smoke emissions can be prosecuted

- Control of noxious emissions (other than smoke, dust, grit and fumes) to the atmosphere.

The prosecution of this legislation is based on identifying the cause of any problem and the organisation responsible for that cause.

Water

The disposal of hazardous substances by tipping them down the sink, or by burning in the open, is dangerous, polluting, irresponsible and illegal. The random uncontrolled discharge of even very small quantities of hazardous waste to the drainage system or sewer may cause catastrophic effects, not only to any water sources but also to their biological equilibrium and to the various stages during the treatment of sewerage and water.

There is also the possibility of water-insoluble substances, such as oils, aggregating and leading to seriously toxic conditions.

Solvents should never be disposed of to a sewer; small amounts of waste should be collected and stored in a proper container for subsequent proper disposal. However, when collecting liquid wastes, care must be taken not to mix liquids which are not compatible. If it is necessary to consider the option of disposing of some liquid waste down the sewer, the organisation must contact the relevant sewerage undertaker *before taking action.*

The **Water Industry Act 1989** was responsible for restructuring the water industry, the privatisation of water companies and the creation of Ofwat (Office of Water Services).

As far as businesses are concerned, the more relevant piece of legislation is the **Water Resources Act 1991**. For occupiers of trade premises, this law allows them to discharge trade effluent into public sewers, provided that the consent of the sewerage undertaker has been obtained. Consents may be subject to the following conditions:

- Which sewer the effluent is discharged into
- The nature or composition of the effluent
- The maximum daily volume and rate of flow
- The time of day when the discharge occurs
- The exclusion of condensing water from the effluent
- The removal or reduction of specified constituents from the effluent
- The temperature and pH (acidity) of the effluent
- Charges payable to the sewerage undertaker for accepting and disposing of the effluent
- Providing and maintaining facilities to allow sampling of the effluent at any time
- Providing, maintaining and testing equipment to measure the volume and rate of discharge and to test the nature and composition of the effluent
- Record keeping relating to the above.

In summary, the business must provide the sewerage undertaker with information on the volume, rate, nature and composition of the effluent.

Those businesses which have a 'consent to discharge' can only apply this consent to the particular effluent specified in the application; if there are any changes, then the consent has to be revised.

Trade effluent is defined in the Act as:

> '... any liquid, either with or without suspended particles, which is produced wholly or partly in the course of any trade or industry carried on at trade premises.'

There are other specific pieces of water legislation which relate to other surface waters and to bathing waters. Overall, the objective of the water legislation is to bring about a range of high-quality waters in rivers, lakes and coastal waters so that the fish and other animals and plants can exist in a stable ecosystem.

Surface water drainage

It is an offence to pollute controlled waters either *deliberately or accidentally*.

Surface water drainage discharges to a watercourse or to groundwater via a soakaway, and surface water drains should therefore carry only uncontaminated rainwater from roofs and clean yard areas. A discharge of waste water to the surface water drain will result in pollution.

In addition, the formal consent of the Environment Agency is required for many discharges to controlled waters, including both direct discharges and discharges to soakaways. Such consents are granted subject to conditions being met and are not granted automatically.

Surface water drains should be identified and marked as such. Existing and new installations such as showers, sinks, laboratories, washdown areas and gullies should be connected to the foul drains – and not just the nearest drain which is often the surface water drain. Oil separators are used to prevent oil entering the water system.

One important step which your business could take is to colour-code all the drain covers on your site. Surface water drains which go into a river (or are otherwise not treated) should be marked green or have a fish painted on them. For the foul drains a red colour might be used. Ensure you back this up with proper training and information to all staff – but especially those most likely to dispose of liquids.

2.2.6 Contaminated land

In the late 1990s, the law relating to the contamination of land was considerably strengthened. The definition of contaminated land is:

> '... land which presents a threat of death, serious injury, or clinical toxicity to humans or a significant threat to ecosystems and property.'

One important aspect of the Environmental Protection Act is that your business must know and record what materials have been put on to your land. It is then a legal requirement to declare this information in the event of your selling the land, and the law makes it clear that it is the company directors who have personal responsibility for this.

2.2.7 Landfill Tax

Strictly speaking, this is a tax rather than controlling legislation. However, the establishment of an organised system for waste disposal permitted the application of a means of collecting a tax related to the amount of waste being disposed of. The implications for businesses are discussed in Chapter 3 on Waste; the categories of waste are detailed in section 3.2.1.

Rates of tax

Date of change	Standard rate £ per tonne	Lower rate £ per tonne
01.10.96	7	2
01.04.99	10	2
01.04.00	11	2
01.04.01	12	2
01.04.02	13	2
01.04.03	14	2
01.04.04	15	2

In the budget of 2003, the Government announced that the standard rate of Landfill Tax would increase by £3 per tonne to £18 per tonne in 2005-6 and by at least £3 per tonne in the years thereafter on the way to a medium- to long-term rate of £35 per tonne.

2.2.8 Climate Change Levy (CCL)

This is another fiscal tax based on the principle of 'polluter pays'. It was introduced in 2001 and placed a charge on all organisations that used electricity, gas or coal, (the fossil fuels). It was designed to be neutral for businesses, in that an employers' national insurance was slightly reduced. Therefore, for businesses that wanted to save a significant amount of money, cutting energy usage was an obvious option.

Currently (2004) the Climate Change levy is unchanged from its 2001 level; however, if it looks as though the UK needs to reduce energy consumption further in order to meet the Kyoto accord or other agreements, then the CCL can be expected to rise.

2.2.9 The WEEE Directive

The WEEE Directive is shorthand for two significant pieces of legislation:

- The **Waste Electrical and Electronic Equipment Directive (WEEED)**
- The **Restriction of Hazardous Substances in Electrical and Electronic Equipment (ROHS) Directive**

Both these pieces of legislation became UK law in August 2004 and will come into effect during the following two years.

The WEEE Directive

This comes into force in August 2005. The aim of the legislation is:

- To reduce the waste arising from electrical and electronic equipment
- To improve the environmental performance of all those involved in the life cycle of electrical and electronic equipment.

The directive affects those involved in manufacturing, selling, distributing, recycling or treating electrical and electronic equipment. The electrical goods covered include:

- Household appliances
- IT and telecommunications equipment
- Audio-visual equipment
- Lighting equipment
- Electrical and electronic toys
- Lighting
- Tools
- Leisure and sports equipment
- Medical devices
- Automatic dispensers.

Some key features of the Directive are that:

By 13 August 2005:

- Private householders will be able to return their WEEE to collection facilities free of charge
- Producers (manufacturers, importers, sellers, distributors) will be responsible for financing the collection, treatment, recovery and disposal of WEEE from private households deposited at these collection points

■ Producers will be responsible for financing the collection, treatment, recovery and disposal of WEEE from users other than private householders for products placed on the market after 13 August 2005.

By 31 December 2006:

■ Producers will be required to achieve a series of demanding recovery and recycling targets for different appliances

■ The UK must have reached an average WEEE collection rate of 4kg per household annually.

The ROHS

The aim is to:

■ Protect human health and the environment by restricting the use of certain hazardous substances in new equipment

■ Complement the WEEE Directive.

The ROHS will affect manufacturers, sellers, distributors and recyclers of electrical and electronic equipment containing lead, mercury, cadmium, hexavalent chromium, polybrominated biphenyls, and polybrominate diphenyl ethers.

Key elements

From July 2006 new electrical equipment will not contain the chemicals listed above, but certain specific items of equipment will be exempt.

Both the WEEE Directive and the ROHS Directive are part of a Europe-wide approach to reducing the consumption of expensive materials and to reducing the risk of harm to health and the environment from the chemicals used in this equipment.

It is clear that, initially, there will be a mixture of systems for collection and treatment and recovery, involving the retailers, the local authorities, the waste management companies and new recycling companies.

There is, therefore, the opportunity for new companies to develop expertise in this new market, though this may also be an area in which existing manufacturers develop expertise.

The other trend which is also likely to develop is the pressure for improved design and construction so that the treatment and recovery/recycling operations can be effected as efficiently as possible.

A longer-term scenario might be the development of lease/take back/re-engineer/re-lease schemes, where the retailer retains ownership of the equipment and maintains it for the customer.

2.2.10 Control of Substances Hazardous to Health Regulations 1994, as amended (COSHH)

This places restrictions on the most harmful substances, with regard to their use, storage, manufacture, processing, classification, packaging and labelling.

2.3 The relevance of environmental legislation for business

2.3.1 Keeping up to date

Legitimate businesses are required to operate within the law. It is therefore important that they maintain a list of relevant legislation and appreciate how this impacts on their operation. There are several commercial products available on the market which detail environmental legislation and what its implications are. However, while most of these products are very good in their own right, what most businesses want to know is:

■ What are the pieces of legislation that apply to them specifically

■ What do they need to do to comply with that legislation.

Several websites are listed in the information section at the end of this chapter, together with sites listing specialist air quality consultants. It should be remembered that, although the Environment Agency was set up by the Government to enforce the legislation, it prefers to give businesses help and advice in order to prevent environmental damage occurring in the first place. Therefore one recommendation would be to contact your local Environment Agency office or, in the case of air quality, contact your local authority in order to discuss how your existing or proposed new processes comply with the law.

Most businesses which approach the Environment Agency wanting advice and help will receive a positive response, partly because the Environment Agency realise that it is better to avoid damage to the environment in the first place, rather than prosecute a company for damage which may be difficult to repair. Contacts for the Environment Agency are provided at the end of this chapter.

An alternative is to visit the website specially set up by the Environment Agency to address the particular legislation issues of each business. Visit www.netregs.gov.uk to find out more.

Other steps you could take are to:

■ **Purchase an environmental law manual:** these are available from a range of organisations, several of whom also produce manuals and updates relating to quality management and health and safety management. The advantage of these is that they are detailed and accurate. The disadvantage is that they do not select the relevant legislation for your business sector and so you still have to search through to find what you want – and you still have to interpret the legislation for your particular situation. Croner and Gee are probably the best known on the market but there are many others

- **Contact your trade organisation.** Most trade organisations are very concerned to keep their member companies informed of the relevant legislation; they also interpret it according to your particular industry sector's requirements and practices

- **Obtain information from the web.** This is reasonably quick and usually accurate, though you have no redress if it is wrong; and increasingly, the knowledge is wrapped up with commercial links

- **Contact your local chamber of commerce.** This approach could be helpful, but it may not be able to help with the specifics in your case

- **Private consultant.** Possibly the same as the chamber of commerce but at a considerably additional cost.

2.3.2 The cost of getting it wrong

The environment costs money – and breaking environmental laws costs a lot of money. In a typical four-month period in autumn 2003, the total fines to organisations found guilty of breaking legislation and harming the environment totalled £290,000. Over a year, this amounts to fines in excess of one million pounds – but you must also take into account legal costs, the cost of management time and the potential damage to a company's reputation; in many cases, companies breaching environmental legislation were subsequently obligated to put in place the very measures they had initially avoided.

Consider some of the cases below.

Breaching of a waste management licence
A skip hire company had a waste management licence which, as normal, had a number of conditions attached to it. However, in contravention of these conditions, the company on several occasions burnt some of the waste. The fire caused a member of the public to inform the police, who sent a helicopter to investigate. The Environment Agency prosecuted the company and an employee, who were fined in excess of £20,000.

Odour offences
A company in Scotland was fined £20,000 after failing to control odours from its site. This followed repeated complaints from members of the public and two enforcement notices from SEPA.

Breach of IPPC conditions

A midlands company had an IPPC authorisation but was found guilty of breaching four conditions of this authorisation. Their employees were found not to have received appropriate training, no method statement or risk assessment was provided and other procedures had not been followed. The granting of IPPC authorisation requires companies to confirm that specific procedures will be followed and breaching these is viewed seriously. The company was fined £5,000.

Land contamination

A London company had used an area of land for several years for the storage of waste materials. These were usually stored in skips but also included oil drums and containers of hazardous materials. There was known to be some contamination of the land. The owner sold the land for development but was then charged with not declaring the contamination of the land. He was fined and required to pay the cost for the remediation of the land. (Fines and costs are not known.)

Radioactive offences

A Manchester company used radioactive material for anti-static cleaning of lenses. Some of this material was taken out of production and placed in an unmarked box on the factory floor, and then went missing. The company had only recently taken over from the previous owner of the factory; the radioactive materials were hired from a specialist company which was properly authorised. However, the (new) Manchester company did not have a proper licence, not realising that a licence could not be transferred from one company to another. It was fined £3,000.

Water offences

A housing development company in Wales was found to have polluted a stream with diesel, which was caused by attempting to move a half-full 300-gallon diesel tank using a fork-lift truck. The tank had dropped and split. The cost of the contamination clean-up totalled £18,000 and in addition the company was fined £1,500.

Down the drain: waste offence

A Kent production company was found guilty of pouring toxic and dangerous chemicals down its drains. The Environment Agency tracked river pollution back to a company site and, by checking on the licensed chemical treatment company which was contracted to remove and treat the waste chemicals from the site, the EA was able to show that some 190,000 litres of chemicals could not be accounted for. The production company claimed that it diluted the chemicals before tipping them down the drain. Interestingly, the company used the word 'enviro' in its name! It was fined £50,000.

2.4 The future

Apart from maintaining and understanding what the legislation is and how it applies to your business, it is also important to consider what the legislation changes are likely to be in the next few years. These changes could affect the plans for investment in new equipment.

Nearly all the changes to environmental law emanate from the European Union. The priority issues for the European Union are to limit climate change, protect nature and biodiversity, ensure the sustainable management of resources and waste as well as addressing health and environment issues. Therefore the legislation which comes forth from the EU either directly or via the UK legislation is likely to address these issues and activities which affect these issues.

2.4.1 Future directives

Some of the specific topics to be addressed include:

- **Directive on Batteries and Accumulators and Waste Batteries and Accumulators:** proposes collection targets for waste batteries and the monitoring of nickel cadmium batteries entering the municipal waste stream. It also sets out new specialist treatment and recycling techniques for waste batteries

- **European Directive on Volatile Organic Compounds (VOCs):** limits are to be set on emissions of VOCs arising from the use of solvents in certain paints, varnishes and vehicle refinishing products

- **European Directive on Environmental Damage:** comprehensive liability regime for damage to the environment. Based on the 'polluter pays' principle, it will require public authorities to identify operators whose activity has caused environmental damage (or threatens to cause such damage) and ensure that they either undertake – or finance – preventative or remedial measures.

  'Environmental damage' includes damage to species and natural habitats protected under European legislation, as well as damage to water resources and land contamination

- **Detergents:** European legislation covering detergents, which dates back to 1973, is to be brought up to date following the adoption of a new European Regulation, which will come into force in October 2005

- **Emissions from off-road machinery:** proposed Directive for the reduction of emissions from engines in non-road mobile machinery.

2.4.2 Water quality

The Commission is currently drawing up a Water Quality Framework Directive which will provide the basis of all future water legislation.

2.4.3 Ecolabels

Ecolabels is the EU approach to providing information on the environmental impacts caused by producing or using a product. They are voluntary, but in some markets they are becoming an important competitive factor. There are many different labelling programs, run by governments, private companies and non-governmental organisations. Take-up of this scheme throughout the EU has been patchy to date, so it is possible that the EU will act to make ecolabels compulsory. See Chapter 8 for more information on this.

2.5 List of environmental legislation

This is a list of the major pieces of legislation that impinge on the environmental aspects of business and commercial activity, as at the end of 2004. It is subject to rapid change.

- Clean Air Act 1993

- Controlled Waste (Registration of Carriers and Seizure of Vehicles) Regulations 1991

- Control of Asbestos in the Air Regulations 1990

- Control of Substances Hazardous to Health Regulations 1994, (as amended) (COSHH)

- Environment Act 1995

- Environmental Protection Act 1990 (Part I: Integrated Pollution Control) (as amended by the Environment Act 1995); (Part II: Waste on Land); (Part III: Statutory Nuisance)

- Environmental Protection (Controls on substances that deplete the ozone layer) Regulations 1996

- Environmental Protection (Duty of Care) Regulations 1991

- Environmental Protection (Prescribed Processes and Substances) Regulations 1991

- Groundwater Regulations 1998

- Landfill Tax Regulations 1996

- Packaging (Essential Requirements) Regulations 1998

- Planning (Control of Major Accident Hazards) Regulations 1999

- Pollution Prevention & Control Regulations 2000 (PPC)

- Producer Responsibility Obligations (Packaging Waste) Regulations 1997 (as amended)

- Special Waste Regulations 1996 (as amended)

- Waste Electrical and Electronic Equipment Directive 2003 (WEEED)

- Waste Management Licensing Regulations 1994

- Water Industry Act 1991

- Water Resources Act 1991

We suggest you note any changes or revised directives of which you become aware, or by-laws which may be aplicable to you.

2.6 Sources of information

Cordis   Community Research and Development
                              Information Service. Up-to-date information
                              about Europe, legislation and funding
                              opportunities.
                              www.cordis.lu

Environment Agency   Official government website with access to
                              vast range of information on the topic. (See
                              also SEPA below)
                              www.environment-agency.gov.uk

European Union   Main access site into all the information,
                              including legislation from the EU. Chose
                              your language from the home page, and then
                              select 'Environment' from the 'Activities' tab.
                              www.europa.eu.int

NetRegs   Part of the Environment Agency, this site
                              provides simple guidance on environmental
                              legislation, and how to comply with it.
                              This site should be your first point of contact
                              to check current legislation.
                              www.netregs.gov.uk

Scottish Environmental Protection Agency (SEPA)
                              www.sepa.org.uk

3

Part 2: The issues

Waste

Case study

Bell Brush Ltd is a small company with 12 employees, in business since the late 1920s. It is a wholesale distributor of a range of cleaning products including brooms, litter pickers, shovels, tools and signs. As a result of its awareness of environmental legislation and its obligations, Bell Brush undertook the following initiatives:

- Reuse of office paper for drafts, memos, messages and calculations – and then shredding this reused paper for use as packaging material
- Reuse of cardboard where possible
- Reuse or recycling of boxes and packaging material
- Consideration of reducing the overlap shrink-wrapping of pallets.
- Requests to its suppliers to:
    - supply goods in reusable and refillable packaging
    - reduce packaging by volume and weight.

CESMB helped it examine its waste and, by cutting out paper, boxes and plastic containers, the company achieved a 50% reduction in its waste disposal costs – and saved a similar amount on packaging costs within two months.

3.1 Overview

Waste is one of the biggest environmental issues we currently face in the UK. We used to think that we needed to cut down on our consumption of natural resources because they would soon run out. Although this is still true, it has rapidly become apparent that we need to cut down on our consumption of virgin natural resources because we are running out of space – landfill – in which to put these resources when we have finished with them.

Not only are we producing more waste than we have space in the ground in which to dump it, but much of that waste is potentially a useful resource. There are metals, organic waste and liquids which could all be reused, thus saving on the landfill space and reducing the need for ever-more virgin resources.

Originally, many of the landfill pits in the UK were a by-product of gravel extraction, open coal quarries or other mineral extraction industries. Now, however, these minerals are not being extracted at the same rate, or alternative materials are being developed. Consequently, there are fewer holes in the UK ground which can be used for landfill.

A third issue is that some material in the landfills – notably the organic matter – decays and gives off methane and carbon dioxide, both of which contribute to global warming. Additionally, some of the liquids in landfill sites can percolate into the groundwater, causing serious pollution problems. This is more likely with older landfill sites but there is always a risk, even with newer sites.

Why do we generate waste?

There are a number of reasons why we generate so much waste. First of all, Britain is an advanced, developed and economically strong country. We are a wealthy society, enjoy a relatively high standard of living and consume large quantities of energy and materials. Moreover, businesses are spending increasing amounts on packaging because it is believed that, in this competitive business world, a product with better packaging sells more.

For example, when we buy a simple muffin, it often comes wrapped in paper, sealed in a plastic bag and finally put in a fancy paper bag. This is not only a waste of natural resources; it also makes the product more expensive for the customer. We have, in the past, taken our natural resources and environment for granted – we simply haven't been aware of the true costs of the waste we generate.

3.2 What is 'waste'?

Over the past twenty years, common terms which have increasingly become matters of concerns are *waste generation* and *waste management*. Both of these terms focus on the word 'waste', so a definition of that would be helpful to start our consideration of this topic.

The legal definition of waste comes from Section 75(2) of the Environmental Protection Act 1990 (EPA 1990), which defines waste 'as any substance or object laid down [in Schedule 2B] which the holder discards, intends to discard or is required to discard'.

The categories laid down in Schedule 2B are:

- Production of consumption residues
- Off-spec products
- Products past their expiry date
- Materials split apart, lost or having undergone mishap including materials, equipment etc contaminated as a result
- Contaminated or soiled materials as a result of planned action
- Contaminated or soiled materials as a result of remedial action (on land)
- Unusable parts
- Substances which no longer perform satisfactorily
- Residues resulting from
    - industrial process
    - pollution abatement processes
    - machining or finishing
    - raw material extraction or processing
- Contaminated materials
- Any substances, products or materials banned by law
- Unwanted products.

The definitions suggest that *waste* is a material that is totally useless to anyone and *has* to be discarded. Yet businesses are using materials whose use can be avoided in the first place – and, furthermore, many businesses are discarding waste that can be either *reused or recycled*. If use of these materials is *reduced*, it will automatically reduce the amount of waste produced.

3.2.1 Waste management

Disposal of waste is now becoming increasingly costly to businesses, partly because the waste contractors have to pay more to dump waste at landfill sites; partly because they are having to make longer journeys to get to usable landfill sites; and also because the UK Government is imposing a 'landfill tax' on every tonne of waste which businesses send to landfill – and this tax is increasing every year.

Types of waste

Waste is costly – the Landfill Tax

This tax was introduced with three aims: encouraging businesses to produce less waste, recover more value from waste (for example through recycling or composting) and to use more environmentally sound methods of waste disposal such as recycling. The tax applies to active and inert waste, disposed of at a licensed landfill site. There are different rates of tax which apply to the three main types of waste:

- **Inactive (or inert) wastes**, such as building rubble: a lower rate of £2 per tonne (2004 cost)

- **'Other waste'** attracts a standard rate of £13 per tonne (2004 figures). Examples of this waste include domestic refuse, most waste discarded by business and street litter

- **'Special wastes'** and **'hazardous waste'** can cost up to four times the rate for 'other waste'. From 2005 the categories of hazardous and special waste will be combined within a single classification, 'special waste'. Examples of this waste include medical waste, hazardous chemicals and radioactive material.

This has risen, deliberately, since its introduction in 1996, when it was only £7 per tonne. It then went to £10 per tonne and increased at the rate of £1 per tonne per year. The Government has indicated that it expects the Landfill Tax to rise by £3 per tonne each year to a top rate of £35 per tonne.

It is quite clear that your business waste is not only a costly item *now*, but will be getting even more costly in the future – so the sooner you start reducing your waste, the more money you will be saving.

This potential saving has stimulated businesses to look carefully at the waste they send to landfill. In many cases this is done by adopting a waste minimisation strategy which, ideally, starts at the beginning of the production process: it looks at the quantity and type of resources ordered in the first place, and then examines the different process stages to see where materials, or energy, or water could be reduced. In addition to the obvious costs of waste, there are also the costs of the unused resources which are bought; the time, effort and storage of these unused resources; and the costs of disposal of these unused resources. Waste minimisation is, clearly, an excellent example of how good environmental practice can save your business money – at no additional cost.

3.2.2 The waste management hierarchy

There is a hierarchy of waste management, represented by the simple diagram below, which shows that the most effective waste management technique is simply to reduce the amount of material which is purchased.

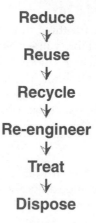

Reduce
↓
Reuse
↓
Recycle
↓
Re-engineer
↓
Treat
↓
Dispose

In terms of your business, you should address each stage of the hierarchy in a logical and considered way, starting with at the top, which is the most straightforward to achieve.

Reduction

If your business were more accurate in its purchasing, you could probably save significant amounts of money: as reduced purchase costs, and as reduced costs for the materials you have bought but have not used, and which now need to be disposed of because they have become damaged or become outdated. Storage and handling costs will also reduce if there is less to store and handle, and associated costs – such as insurance, heating or lighting – may also be lower. These savings, of course, need to be balanced against increased administrative time in reordering, and possible additional transportation requirements.

Reuse

The next best step in waste management for your business is to examine the potential for reuse of materials. One of the best examples is the reuse of cardboard boxes. Many business receive goods in cardboard boxes which they then crush and throw away – but then buy new cardboard boxes in order to despatch their products. This clearly costs money, both in *disposal* costs and additional *purchase* costs. Many businesses now use plastic crates or boxes, which are much more durable and which go back and forth between supplier and customer; although there is an initial investment, the payback time is usually short. In this situation, the supplier benefits as well as the customer, who has less cardboard waste to dispose of.

Case study: the inconsiderate customer
Many businesses report that they are forced to purchase new cardboard boxes because their customers are unwilling to receive goods delivered in old, reused, boxes. It is unclear what the reason for this is, and many businesses have tried to discuss this with their customers, but without success. Since there is a potential saving for both customer and supplier, one can only describe the customer attitude as short-sighted.

Recycle

Recycling has been around for some time but is increasingly being seen as a sound option for waste management. However, businesses need to appreciate that recycling is not necessarily a cheaper alternative to waste disposal. For some materials (such as metals, good-quality paper and glass) good prices can be paid; for other materials (such as paper, card, wood) prices can fluctuate. There are many companies now offering recycling services and it would be sensible to cast around to identify what prices you can get for the different waste materials you generate.

If your business operates on an industrial estate, it would be sensible to collaborate with the other businesses to obtain viable quantities of recyclate for collection, as the output from any single company may require lengthy storage to build up to a minimum collection load. The other side of the recycling coin for your business is the extent to which there might be a business opportunity for you in using recyclate materials to develop new products for your business. Ultimately, the success of recycling will depend, in part, on the extent to which your business, and you personally, purchase products made from recycled materials, as this will help create a market for such items.

Re-engineer

Re-engineering is an even more sophisticated approach to waste management than recycling; in 2004 it was boosted by the implementation of the Waste Electrical and Electronic Equipment (WEEE) Directive, which aims to reduce the quantity of electrical and electronic equipment which is thrown away. When fully implemented, this legislation will, especially where small businesses are concerned, offer a different option to just throwing away their old computers and other electrical equipment; it may also offer a business opportunity for SMEs to show how they could re-engineer some of these items. See Chapter 2 for more information.

Treatment

Treatment of waste usually means that it is incinerated to provide energy. Some businesses which produce a lot of combustible waste material (such as those working with wood) have been using onsite incinerators for many years to power their factory heating. This is an option which many more businesses should consider. Until recently, there were few incinerators in the UK which took waste and produced energy (electricity) to be fed into the national grid, but this situation is now changing.

Disposal

Disposal of waste is the least environmentally sound option – but it is the commonest route in the UK. It is also the cheapest, but that is rapidly changing, as we have seen from the information on the Landfill Tax.

Some facts

Recovery: a recent EU report suggests that the UK recovered 9% of its waste in 1999, the worst in the EU – the best are Germany and Austria, who recover 48%

Landfill: 84% of municipal waste in England and Wales is disposed of to landfill, as at 2004. The EU Directive on landfill requires a reduction in the use of landfill as a means of disposal, to 35% of the 1995 total by 2014. This will lead to a radical reappraisal of waste management solutions and probably a significant increase in 'treatment' and in 'creative' new methods.

Incineration: About 2% of controlled waste is incinerated. This proportion is set to increase, given the need to reduce current reliance on landfill.

At the current rate at which we are using up landfill space, the south-east of the UK has only enough space to last for the next *seven* years.

A best practice office consumes about seven reams of paper per year per employee.

(www.environment-agency.gov.uk) (2003)

3.3 Waste and your business

To get some idea of how much waste is costing your business, carry out this simple task:

- **Step 1:** Browse through your skip on the morning of the day of collection.

- **Step 2:** List the different materials you find in the skip and their approximate quantities.

- **Step 3:** Calculate an approximate value of the materials being discarded.

You will probably find that what is in your skip – ready to be, literally, thrown away without any further thought – adds up to a reasonable sum of money. Your challenge is to see how you can avoid creating much of this waste in the first place, and then to see if you can find a different use for the waste which cannot be avoided.

3.3.1 Where does waste come from?

In 2003, 165m tonnes of controlled waste was produced in England and Wales – 70% of this controlled waste went to the landfill (Source: Environment Agency)

Of the 165m tonnes, 28m tonnes (17%) was municipal solid waste, 67m tonnes (40%) was construction and demolition waste and 70m tonnes (43%) was industrial and commercial waste.

Is *your* business producing waste?

All businesses produce waste. There is no escaping the fact. But the quantities of waste generated are of course different depending on the nature of the business and the waste management strategies adopted by businesses.

It is true that, in most cases, larger-scale enterprises produce more waste than the small and medium-sized enterprises (SMEs). According to the Environment Agency, however, the total amount of waste produced by all SMEs far exceeds the total amount produced by all larger businesses; it is for this reason that the Government is putting financial pressure on all businesses to reduce the amount of waste sent to landfill.

The figure overleaf shows waste production by sector, as extracted from Environment Agency data, 2003.

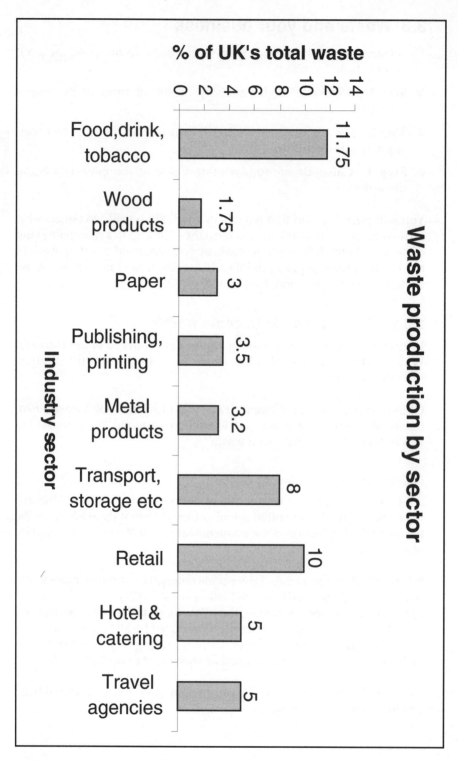

3.3.2 Where does the waste in your business arise?

Waste arises at virtually every stage in a business operation, and comes in three main forms:

■ **Material waste:** this is the waste you can physically touch, such as paper, card, metals or plastics

■ **Energy waste:** this is the waste from lighting, heating and running equipment etc. Studies have shown that, in most organisations, it is possible to save 10% of this energy without any investment, simply by changing the way staff do things. For further information on this area please see Chapter 5

■ **Wasted time:** this is a staff cost and many businesses have tried to address this in recent years – but there is still considerable wastage of staff time in many businesses. This is not a topic which we are addressing directly in this book, but it is an important issue for many organisations, and should not be forgotten.

3.3.3 Calculating the amount of waste in your business

You may well have some idea of where *most* of the waste comes from in your business. However, you may not be aware of all the waste from all the different sections in your business – and you are probably not aware of all the different materials from your business which are disposed of as waste.

The audit form which follows represents a small business and the typical steps that produce waste. You can use this generalised example as a guideline for your business and to identify the various wastes produced at different stages of operation.

A simple way of doing this is a walk-through of the various departments of your business. Use the form while walking through the various operations and note how much waste is generated. We have shown 'paper', 'card', 'metal' and 'plastic', but you may need to alter these headings, add columns for different waste materials, or alter the names and number of departments.

Waste Audit

Department	Paper *weekly qty* *used / wasted*		Cardboard *weekly qty* *used / wasted*		Metal *weekly qty* *used / wasted*		Plastic *weekly qty* *used / wasted*	
Office								
Storage								
Loading bay								
Waste skips								
Processing / Production								
Goods / Packaging								
Total waste per week								
x 52 = total waste per year								

In addition to the data listed here you should also make a list of additional, and occasional, waste items such as toner cartridges, furniture or food – the types of disposal that only take place irregularly, and are unlikely to show up on a 'snapshot' view of the organisation.

Once you have compiled this list, you are in a position to start considering your business in terms of the waste hierarchy described earlier:

- **Reduce:** identify *which* of the wastes you have listed could be reduced – and *how*: by cutting them out altogether, purchase of different materials with less waste or other means

- **Reuse:** which of the wastes listed could be reused – do you use paper on both sides; do you have china mugs in the canteen which can be reused rather than plastic ones; can waste washing water be reused as 'grey water' in the toilet cistern?

- **Recycle:** speak to your waste carrier and find out what waste they will take for recycling and if they want it segregated. If they cannot help, contact a specialist recycling company – there are now plenty in the UK.

Note that it may require several months' notice to change arrangements with your waste carrier should you wish to recycle more, or change carriers

- **Re-engineer:** build up a list of firms that will take old computers, printers and other electrical equipment so that when you have the items for disposal, you have the contacts to hand.

Finance

The other important step within your move to effective waste management is to cost all the expenses – and the savings – so that you know where you are saving money and where you might need to reinvest some of these savings.

> ### Case study: Kardwell Hobbs
> Kardwell Hobbs is a wholesaler of cards, stationery and toys based in Brimsdown, north London.
>
> The main warehouse area is a large open building put up about 20 years ago. Most of the operation took place on the ground floor but there was a small mezzanine area. Heating costs were very high in order to keep the main warehouse area at an acceptable temperature – with the result that the mezzanine area was always very warm. The company did not segregate its waste, which included not only significant quantities of paper and card, but also old fittings and equipment.
>
> In 2003/4 it had a blitz on this approach: the company brought in a metal recycler to remove (and pay for) the old scrap metal and then instituted a recycling collection scheme for all its paper and card.
>
> In addition, it rented off half the warehouse to another company; the income from this allowed it to build another, larger, mezzanine. This has also given the company much better control of the overall temperature in the building.
>
> This approach has focused attitudes on reducing energy costs in the offices: the lights are regularly switched off and heating is usually off because some trickles through from the warehouse area.
>
> Kardwell Hobbs estimates that energy saving and the reduction of waste to landfill has saved approximately £10,000 over the past 12 months.

3.4 Sources of information

ACM Waste plc   Provides recycling services throughout UK, either directly, or through an associate recycling company.
www.acm-waste.com

Aluminium Can Recycling Association
Information on aluminium cans.
www.alupro.org.uk

Chartered Institute of Waste Management
Professional body for waste and resource management. CIWM supplies publications, holds events, provides training etc. on issues related to waste.
www.ciwm.co.uk

Computer Aid   Accepts and donates computers.
www.computer-aid.org

Computers for charity   Free collection of redundant computers.
www.cfcuk.org

Computers for the disabled Accepts computers for recycling.
www.cftd.co.uk

Computer Recycling   Collects computers for recycling.
www.communitytechnology.org.uk

Confederation of Paper Industries
Information on paper – some environmental information.
www.paper.org.uk

Department of Environment, Food and Rural Affairs
Wide-ranging information regarding waste can be found on the Government's official environmental department website.
Tel: 08459-556 000
www.defra.gov.uk/environment/waste/

Industry Council for Electronic Equipment
Business approaches to recycling of electronic equipment.
www.icer.org.uk

Letsrecycle   Website providing information about everything related to waste (legislation, prices, products, WEEE, packaging, landfill, etc.) Additionally, 'club recycle' is a well-known online forum/discussion room for all waste-related issues.
www.letsrecycle.com

NLRF   A steering group as well as online forum to discuss issues related to recycling in north London.
www.scrapp.org.uk/services/forum.html

3

Recycle Now   Ideas on recycling.
www.recyclenow.com

Recycled Products   Wide range of products listed.
www.recycledproducts.org.uk

Recycling information   Useful and interesting site for information.
www.recycle-more.co.uk

Save-a-cup   Organises schemes to recycle vending cups.
www.save-a-cup.co.uk

The Waste Book   Waste management providers for London and the South East.
www.recycle.mcmail.com

The Waste Guide   Extremely comprehensive selection of waste and recycling references and contacts.
www.wasteonline.org.uk/resources/
Wasteguide/mn_references.html

Tools for Schools   Accepts computers.
www.tfs.org.uk

WasteWatch   Working with businesses in certain areas to assist in waste minimisation and recycling of waste.
www.wastewatch.org.uk

Packaging

Case study

Colin Clapp Direct Mail, a large printing operation in Hoddesdon, Herts, used large quantities of cardboard boxes – from incoming goods, for outgoing goods and also for internal movements of stock. By unpacking the incoming boxes more carefully, it was able to save significant sums of money by reusing these boxes for the internal movements. It also invested in flexible packaging which can be reused over a longer period of time.

4.1 Overview

During the past twenty years, there has been a considerable expansion in the amount and type of packaging used for an increasingly wide range of products. Nearly all of this packaging ends up in landfill and adds significantly to the overall waste disposal problems of the UK.

The reason for this increase in packaging is, primarily, due to two pressures:

- **To protect food products and potentially dangerous equipment.** This has come about because of health concerns and in most situations is difficult to argue against

- **For marketing and sales purposes.** These reasons include ease of access on display shelves, protection of fragile equipment, prevention of pilfering and containment of goods during their transportation.

Packaging is made up of a wide variety of materials with plastics, cardboard and paper being the most frequently used type of material. The problem with some of these materials is that plastics are very difficult to recycle, because of the wide variety of plastic actually used. The difficulty in separating them means that collecting and recycling present several practical problems. However, for businesses which have restricted types of plastic packaging, this may be possible. Although it is of course possible to recycle cardboard, much is 'contaminated' with sticky tapes, glue, staples and printing inks. Efforts are being made to recycle cardboard effectively, but the very high volumes produced mean that there is a 'cardboard mountain' to deal with.

In 1997, the Government introduced the **Producer Responsibility Obligations (Packaging Waste) Regulations**, usually referred to, more simply, as 'the Packaging Regulations'. This was an industry-developed scheme, designed to identify the different stages involved in packaging goods and then to allocate responsibility to businesses involved in the different stages of using packaging, for reduction and recycling. This meant that all businesses involved in producing packaging materials, as well as those involved in filling the packaging and disposing of it, have a responsibility to recycle or recover an identified percentage.

In the context of the Packaging Regulations, packaging includes not only plastics, cardboard, paper and those other materials we might normally think of as 'packaging', but also glass bottles, which may be filled with a product; wooden containers; and the metal or polypropylene strapping and tie systems used to contain materials.

Case study: The cardboard box buyer

This company distributes clothing to its shops throughout the UK; it is primarily a retail clothing company – buying from a variety of manufacturers, both in the UK and abroad. The clothing supplies arrive at the warehouse in cardboard boxes of various sizes. The clothes are then sorted into different ranges as required by the company's different shops, then packed in new and larger cardboard boxes for distribution; a contract carrier is used for the purpose.

All the cardboard boxes which arrive from the suppliers are flattened and disposed of through the company's normal waste carrier; this amounts to about two skips per week, at an average cost of about £150. The cost of the new, larger, cardboard boxes is, on average, £1,000 per week. The company doesn't repack into the boxes which arrive from the supplier as the contract with its carrier is per box, NOT by weight, so the larger boxes keep the transport costs down. It would seem sensible to renegotiate the transport contract in order to allow the use of two or three of the suppliers' (smaller) boxes; this should largely eliminate the purchase of new boxes, and considerably reduce the amount, and cost, of waste disposal.

This case is a classic example of an organisation costing each part of the business operation separately and not looking at the overall process, nor examining different approaches which, overall, may be less costly. 'Not seeing the wood for the trees' or 'not seeing the big picture' are frequent comments used about waste management.

4.2 The packaging issue

4.2.1 What is packaging?

The 1997 Regulations define packaging as: 'all products made of any material of any nature to be used for the containment, protection, handling, delivery and presentation of goods, from raw materials to processed goods, from the producer to the user or the consumer, including non-returnable items used for the same purpose'.   This definition is applicable only where the products are:

■ **Primary packaging (sales).** This refers to packaging conceived so as to constitute a sales unit to the final user or consumer at the point of purchase, such as a crisp packet

■ **Secondary packaging (grouped).** This comprises packaging which groups a number of items together at the point of purchase. It can be removed from the product without affecting its characteristics, such as the box in which packets of crisps are supplied to retailers

- **Tertiary packaging (transport).** This aspect of packaging, which could include pallets, facilitates handling and transport of a number of sales units or grouped packaging, in order to minimise damage arising out of physical handling and transport. It does not include road, rail, ship and air containers.

'Packaging' therefore includes items such as boxes, pallets, tubes, bags, sacks; the items may be made out of paper, board, glass, metals, plastics, ceramics or other materials. 'Packaging' can also include tape, wrapping, binding and tying materials.

4.2.2 Environmental impact of packaging

Packaging has a range of environmental impacts: both the use of resources and energy in its manufacture, and the use of transport in carrying the packaging to the site of use. The other major impact of packaging is the waste and disposal. In the UK, around 12 million tonnes of packaging waste are disposed of each year, most going to landfill. The other way in which packaging can have a environmental impact is through the level of protection afforded to the goods. Packaging which is inadequate in quantity or type can lead to loss or damage of the goods themselves, causing greater wastage. Over-packaging is also an issue, in that it usually leads to a greater quantity of waste materials.

The particular design and type of material used for packaging plays an important role in influencing the impact of packaging on the environment:

- The **raw material** of the packaging can affect the waste disposal and also the potential for recycling. In addition, where packaging is composed of more than one type of material, the recycling process is much more difficult; where cardboard and plastic are combined, for example, they can be difficult to separate and recycle

- The **quantity of raw material** is also an issue. Most manufacturers prefer to keep packaging to a minimum, where possible, in order to minimise costs. One-way-trip packaging, reduced to a minimum, runs the risk of not offering sufficient protection and could actually generate more waste through damage to goods. However, using more durable packaging or returnable packaging does offer more protection – but at a higher cost and requiring the awareness (and willingness) of the customer to return the packaging

- The third environmental issue concerned with packaging is the **energy usage**. Energy is inherent within the product, but it is also part of the *production* of the packaging itself, the *transport* of the packaging, and in the *transport* of the packaged product: products with greater amounts of packaging require greater space or weight, thus requiring more energy.

The best practical environmental options for packaging are, therefore, to:

- Use packaging which is reusable over and over again
- Purchase one-way packaging made from recycled materials
- Dispose of end-of-life packaging in any way except landfill.

Case study: Cable Drums

This small north London company specialises in the purchase and redistribution of electrical cable of all types, to a wide range of purchasers, including utility companies and DIY stores. The cabling arrives on very large wooden reels and is then rewound onto either medium or small wooden reels, depending on the customer's order. Originally, the company purchased new reels for this purpose, the medium-sized reels costing £9 each and the smaller reels £3. It was then left to the customers to dispose of the old reels. Following the introduction of the Landfill Tax [see Chapter 2 for more information] and the Packaging Directive, the company started to work with its contract transport provider and its customers. For each medium-sized reel that was returned, the customer received £2 and the transport firm received £1; for each small reel returned, the customer received 75p and the transport company 25p. Every organisation in this supply chain benefited: the cable company was significantly reducing its costs by not having to buy new reels, the transport company was getting some costs for its return journey and the customer was not having to pay for the disposal of the old reels. In addition, there was environmental benefit from using fewer trees to manufacture additional reels and the landfill was reduced, with the subsequent reduction of methane and CO_2 resulting from the decay of the wood.

4.2.3 The packaging process

The packaging life cycle consists of the following stages:

- **Manufacturing packaging raw materials,** such as manufacture of plastic granules, paper, or aluminium sheets
- **Converting packaging,** such as converting plastic granules into food trays, paper into cardboard or aluminium into drink cans and the associated printing
- **Filling packaging with goods,** such as food onto to plastic trays, drink into cans
- **Wholesaling,** such as a wholesaler supplying packaged goods to a shop
- **Selling to final user,** such as selling food or drink across the counter to final customer.

4.2.4 The Producer Responsibility Obligations (Packaging Waste) Regulations 1997

The objectives of the regulations are:

- To achieve a more sustainable approach to dealing with packaging waste

- To reduce the amount of packaging going to landfill

- To implement the recovery and recycling targets in the EC Directive on Packaging and Packaging Waste, which specifies that at least 50% of all packaging waste should be recovered, and at least 25% should have been recycled by 2001. These percentages are likely to increase over the coming decade.

The regulations respond to UK industry's requests to have:

- Legislative underpinning for recovery and recycling obligations in order to deter 'free riders'

- Business-led collective schemes, to discharge businesses' obligations for them

- An approach which shares the recovery and recycling obligation between all parts of the packaging chain.

4.2.5 Who is obligated?

The obligation to respond to the Packaging Waste Regulations applies to any person who performs an activity and supplies packaging, with or without a product inside it, to the next stage in the packaging chain or to the final user of the packaging. The obligation applies to businesses that perform one or more of the following stages:

- Manufacturing packaging raw materials

- Converting materials into packaging

- Packing and filling packaging

- Selling packaging to the final user.

There is also the need to pass two threshold tests to determine if a business is obligated; **both** tests must apply:

- A turnover of **more than £2 million** in the last financial year

- Handling **more than 50 tonnes of packaging** or packaging material in the previous year.

4.2.6 What does obligation involve?

The regulations impose three main obligations on business:

■ **Registration** obligation

■ **Recovery and recycling** obligation

■ **Certifying** obligation.

These are now looked at in some greater detail.

Registration obligation

This requires the business to register with the Environment Agency (EA) (or the Scottish Environmental Protection Agency (SEPA), for Scotland). This involves the payment of a fee and the declaration of the packaging data on a form. The (current) deadline for annual registration is 7 April.

Recovery and recycling obligation

Businesses are obliged to take reasonable steps to recover and recycle a specific tonnage of packaging waste, calculated on the basis of three factors:

■ The tonnage of packaging handled by the business in the previous year

■ The 'activities' that the business performs and the percentage obligation attached to each activity. (The packaging life cycle has been split into clear sections described above and the percentage role of packaging at each stage has been estimated.)

■ The national recovery and recycling targets.

Certifying obligation

Obligated businesses have to certify that they have recovered and recycled the necessary tonnage of packaging waste. This is done by writing to the relevant agency by 31 January following the end of the calendar year in which it is obligated.

The legislation does not explain how obligated producers should go about taking their 'reasonable steps' to meet the targets and so the Government created the Packaging Waste Recovery Notes system (PRNs).

4.2.7 What are PRNs?

PRNs are uniquely numbered documents supplied by the Environment Agency (or SEPA in Scotland) to accredited reprocessors, and show that reprocessing of a certain tonnage of packaging waste has taken place. PRNs are tradeable, their price is determined by market forces and they can be purchased by anyone.

Sometimes PRNs are also referred to as 'evidence of compliance'. The reprocessor can issue a PRN to certify that a certain tonnage of post-use packaging waste, arising in the UK, has been recycled or recovered. Obligated companies, their representatives and compliance schemes (on behalf of their members) purchase this evidence to demonstrate that their obligations under the regulations have been discharged.

The sale of PRNs by reprocessors generates revenue which should be used to provide incentives to increase the quantities of UK packaging waste being collected, reprocessed and sold. The money that members pay to compliance schemes to offset their obligations is therefore used to purchase PRNs and support the relevant activities, ensuring that compliance schemes can meet their obligations in future years, when the recovery targets increase. Information on locating compliance schemes is provided at the end of the chapter.

How is the price of PRNs determined?

The price of the PRN is related to the price of the recyclable commodity. In the short term, a surplus of demand for PRNs over supply will keep the PRN prices high, whereas a surplus of recyclable commodities over demand will keep commodity prices low. If the price for the commodity increases, so the PRN availability will increase and the PRN price will decrease – and vice versa. But in the Packaging Waste Regulations there is a material-specific recycling requirement and a general recovery and recycling requirement for which a PRN of any material can be used. Hence the value of the PRN of any individual material is not *solely* dependent on the price of the commodity but also on the general availability of PRNs – this will tend to dampen the fluctuations in PRN prices. Certainly, until there is an overall surplus of PRNs, prices will tend to remain high. For this complex balance to be achieved there needs to be a central market place for PRNs.

How to obtain PRNs

PRNs can be obtained by three methods:

- By recovering and recycling a sufficient quantity of packaging yourself

- By linking with another business that is able to recover and recycle enough packaging to satisfy its own and other business requirements for PRNs. (This method could become risky should the Government increase the number of PRNs required or if PRNs no longer become available for the supplementing business.)

- By buying from the Environment Exchange.

What is the Environment Exchange (EE)?

The Environment Exchange provides an open and auditable electronic trading facility for PRNs recyclable commodities and future contracts in these commodities. Contact information can be found at the end of the chapter.

It should be noted that there is no charge to join EE, nor, if you do join, is there any obligation to buy and sell all your PRNs through EE.

4.2.8 The Environment Agency's powers

The EA (or SEPA in Scotland) has a duty to monitor compliance by producers, against their obligations under the regulations. In this respect they have the same sort of powers of entry and inspection as they have for their other environmental duties. The agencies are also required to maintain a public register, publish their monitoring programmes and report half-yearly on number, size and sector of businesses monitored for registration, data and compliance with recovery and recycling obligations.

The Packaging (Essential Requirements) Regulations 1998

The Packaging (Essential Requirements) Regulations 1998 implement the single-market provisions of the EC Directive on Packaging and Packaging Waste. They require certain conditions to be met in relation to the manufacture and composition of packaging and to its reusability and recoverability. The essential requirements basically consist of:

- Reducing packaging volume and weight

- Limiting the use of hazardous substances

- Designing packaging suitable for recovery and recycling.

Common criticisms

The compliance scheme was originally set up by industry representatives responding to Government requests for industry to tackle the ever-growing mountain of packaging waste. One of the common criticisms of the scheme is that companies obligated to recycle their packaging can avoid doing anything different – other than purchase PRNs to cover the amount of packaging waste which they should recycle. They can then carry on piling their waste packaging into skips and pay for skips to be taken away. Such a step does nothing to reduce the amount of packaging waste going to landfill – and does nothing to help your company save money.

The danger for your business of pursuing this option is that the price of PRNs can fluctuate, and it is more likely to fluctuate up than down. This is because companies able to recycle their own waste are better off using the 'individual route' (see next page) rather than joining a compliance scheme, thus resulting in an increasing number of companies wanting PRNs but not actually carrying out recycling of packaging.

4.3 What your business needs to do

If your business is an 'obligated producer' of packaging according to the definitions provided earlier, note that it will be a criminal offence to fail to meet your three obligations of registration, recovery and certification, or to provide false or misleading data to the agencies.

You have three methods of complying with the regulations:

- **Individual route:** the producer (your business) discharges its obligations itself, in which case it must: register with the relevant agency; pay a fee (currently £768); provide packaging data; carry out the necessary recovery and recycling; and provide a certificate of compliance to the agency.

   The documented evidence could be in the form of packaging recovery notes (PRNs) issued by the organisation(s) that perform the recovery and recycling operations for you (i.e. the accredited reprocessor(s)).

   If you cannot obtain PRNs from an accredited reprocessor for any reason, or if you are unable to meet your obligation for other reasons, you can purchase PRNs on the open market to cover the percentage of your obligation. The Environment Agency will be able to provide you with details of organisations from which you can purchase bona fide PRNs. To meet your obligations there are two available routes:

   - **using your own packaging waste:** you can discharge your obligation by recycling packaging waste that arises at your backdoor: that is, transit packaging discarded around goods you receive. You need to know how much is 'packaging waste' and how much is 'general waste' – an important distinction, as you can only discharge your obligation with packaging waste. If registered as a group, you can combine *all* of the group's packaging waste
   - **meeting your obligation externally:** if you have a deficit that you need to meet externally, you need to obtain evidence that recovery has happened on your behalf. There is plenty of scope for imagination on the forging of partnerships, trading etc to obtain packaging waste, or to ensure it is recycled on your behalf

- **Collective scheme:** the producers will be exempt from complying with their legal obligations for that year. They are only required to pay the fee and provide packaging data to the scheme. If any business provides false or misleading information to a scheme, it can be ejected from membership and would then be open to prosecution

- **Setting up your own compliance scheme:** this option may offer a cost-effective solution in some situations. If members (from your local area, industrial estate, business club etc) are carefully chosen, you can:
   - pool your backdoor packaging waste arisings
   - share collection costs
   - negotiate as a group with reprocessors.

In all cases, producers have to keep records of certain information regarding the recovery and recycling undertaken. If any of the foregoing schemes, individual or collective, fail to comply, they may be liable to prosecution for criminal offences.

4.3.1 Compliance schemes

A compliance scheme is an organisation that has been authorised to take over the legal responsibilities of its members with regards to the Packaging Regulations. The advantages of joining a compliance scheme are twofold:

- The individual businesses are exempted from legal obligation

- The risk of non-compliance, which businesses face if attempting to comply on an individual basis, is removed.

Variations in charging systems

There is considerable variation in compliance scheme charges. In general, a scheme's membership fee is particularly significant for businesses with small annual tonnage obligations. For example, a firm with a high annual turnover and low tonnage obligation of, say, 100 tonnes could reduce compliance costs significantly by choosing a scheme with a low membership fee.

As a company's tonnage obligation increases, the PRN levy rates charged by schemes become more important, and a firm with an obligated tonnage of several thousand tonnes will find that the PRN levies are the dominant cost factor.

Operation method

Although each compliance scheme sets up its own method of operation, there are some common characteristics in the way they are run:

- Compliance schemes agree contracts with reprocessors, who can provide legally acceptable evidence that recovery and recycling of stated tonnages of qualifying packaging waste has taken place to meet member obligations. Sometimes these contracts also involve other parties, such as local authorities and waste management companies

- Compliance schemes should ensure that contracts stimulate investment in the collection and recovery processes in order to increase capacities and thus meet the regulatory targets. Nevertheless, the reality is somewhat different and reprocessors have been criticised for not investing PRN sales in recycling projects

- Each material stream, such as paper, card or plastics, has its own characteristics and difficulties. It is sometimes necessary to incentivise the collection of packaging waste which is currently unprofitable. Compliance schemes are supposed to play an active role in stimulating the market, for example by supporting investment when there is a shortage of reprocessing capacity or through finding new uses for recycled products.

4.3.2 The steps to take

If you believe that your business falls within the requirements to recycle packaging, i.e. you are obligated, there are several steps you should take:

- Check the amount of packaging which constitutes your waste: you could do this by asking your waste carrier to do it for you, or by recording the amount of packaging waste disposed of by your business each week or month and multiplying up from there

- If you decide that your business is obligated, contact the Environment Agency and obtain their current advice

- If your packaging waste is largely of one type of material, such as cardboard, it is probably most cost-effective for you to collect that all together, compact it and sell it direct to a reprocessor. When speaking to the reprocessor find out not only the *current* price for the material but also how it tends to *fluctuate*

- If your packaging waste is of several types you will need to decide how easy it is to separate it into the different constituents and whether you have sufficient space to store the different containers

- As you recycle this packaging waste you should receive PRNs from the Environment Agency. You can then see if you can sell these to the compliance organisations or other companies.

In summary

The Packaging Regulations were put in place to try to reduce the amount of packaging waste which was being produced. They are relatively complex and are administratively difficult to follow, but businesses who can apply the time to the scheme can potentially save considerable sums of money.

4.4 Sources of information

Environment Exchange PRNs and packaging support.
www.t2e.co.uk   Tel: (020) 7815 3879

Environmentally sound packaging
Good independent source of information.
www.wasteonline.org.uk

Environmental Packaging
Producers of reduced-impact packaging
www.friendlypackaging.org.uk

European Organisation for Packaging and the Environment
Interesting issues.
www.europen.be

HMSO Legislation page Official document regarding the Producer
Responsibility Obligations (Packaging Waste
Legislation) 1997
www.legislation.hmso.gov.uk/si/si1997/
1970648.htm

Institute of Environmental Management and Assessment
Regularly updated website about Producer
Responsibility and Packaging Regulation.
Also provides a range of publications.
www.iema.net/htmlpage.php?pid=155

Industry Council for Packaging and the Environment
Useful information
www.incpen.org

Kite Environmental Solutions
Information and support about Packaging
Waste Regulations
www.kitepackaging.co.uk/new/
regulations.html

The Onyx Group Information and FAQs about Packaging
Waste Regulations
www.onyxgroup.co.uk/pages/
opguidetoregs.asp

Packaging Compliance Schemes
Go to an internet search engine and type in
"Packaging Compliance Schemes UK"

Packaging **Magazine** Magazine site – useful articles.
www.packagingmagazine.co.uk

Science Year Education site but good examples of peoples
response to packaging.
www.scienceyear.com/outthere/environment

Tetra Pak Company site but some useful comments
about packaging. Look at 'Tetra Pak and the
Environment' once you access the home page.
www.tetrapakusa.com

Energy

5

Case study

Grobern Graphics, a small design and specialist printing company in Broxbourne, Herts, decided in 1999 that it would try to reduce energy costs. The company used electricity for lighting and machine operation and gas for heating. During the six summer months it reduced gas consumption to zero, and halved electricity consumption; over the whole year average gas consumption fell by 65%. The company had achieved this simply by persuading staff to do things differently, wear warmer clothes, switch off lights and machines, including computers when not in use for more than 30 minutes. The saving was a few hundred pounds but for a small company it made a big difference.

5.1 Overview

We are using more and more energy in our everyday lives, at work and at home. Although much of the equipment and machinery we use is increasingly more energy efficient, we are using more powered equipment to perform tasks which we used to perform manually. In the UK, most of this energy comes from burning fossil fuels, mostly natural gas or oil. This, in turn, is contributing to global warming. Although the UK generates some of its energy requirements from nuclear power, the nuclear stations are coming to the end of their life and all are likely to be closed down by 2020. We are investing in wind turbines, but the landscape impact of these is causing many communities to object strongly to them; a very small amount of energy is harnessed from solar power.

Most energy supply in the UK comes from oil and gas from the North Sea, though we still have a reliance on oil from the Middle East. Supplies from the North Sea are estimated to have about 15-20 years of life left, but well before then we will need to buy oil and gas supplies from elsewhere in the world; Russia is currently being investigated as a likely option. Wherever we get these energy supplies from, there is likely to be some concern about political stability and the impact of terrorism, so it is important that, in the UK, we have a range of energy materials and sources and do not depend too much on a single source or single type of energy.

As well as being concerned about where our future energy supplies will come from, we also need to be concerned about the impact of burning fossil fuels (coal, gas and oil) which provide us with electricity. Data indicates that over the past 150 years the global temperature has risen by approximately 0.5⁰C.

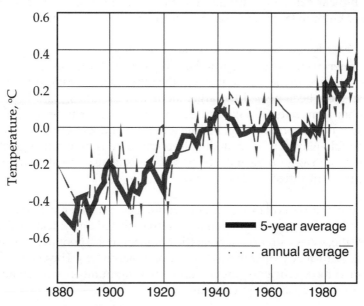

Other data also shows that the concentration of carbon dioxide in the atmosphere has risen from 265ppm (parts per million) in 1850 to 370ppm in 2001 and could rise to 600ppm by 2060.

Most scientists accept that this increased level of carbon dioxide has arisen from the burning of fossil fuels and there is a broad acceptance that this has caused the increased global temperature – though it is fair to say that many in the oil, coal and gas companies do not agree with this analysis.

In the late 1980s, the UK Government took the strategic decision that it should err on the side of caution and adopt the precautionary principle that – even if the global temperature rise were *not* due to burning fossil fuels – it would be better to take steps to reduce energy consumption because the long-term consequences of not doing so would place very serious pressures on all of us. Many other governments around the world have adopted the same precautionary approach.

It is therefore clear that, in the UK, it is highly likely that the cost of electricity and other energy will rise steadily over the next few years in an attempt to encourage people and businesses to be more careful about their use of energy. In 2004, the first indications of these increased costs was seen as the main power supply companies all raised their tariffs.

5.2 Energy: the real issues

Energy consumption in the UK is growing, mainly because we are using an ever-increasing range of machinery and equipment which uses electrical power rather than being manual, hydraulic or oil-powered. As far as typical company offices are concerned, the use of electrically-powered equipment has increased steadily over the past 20 years.

In the 1980s, typewriters were manual or required low electrical power; photocopiers were less common and used sparingly; there was no separate printer attached to the typewriter. On the other hand, the old office was likely to have been heated by large, inefficient radiators, and lighting was either from natural daylight, from strip lights or tungsten bulbs. There was no air conditioning, but the windows and walls were unlikely to be double-glazed or insulated. Although there is now much greater efficiency of usage, on balance today's office is using a great deal more energy than the office of 20 years ago.

Many similar aspects of energy usage would have been seen in the typical home of 20 years ago, with the same pattern repeated on the factory floor – where there was a great deal of inefficient machinery, poor lighting and heating, with many operations being done manually. These are now performed more efficiently, but by an increasing number of machines – of increasingly great power consumption.

We cannot go back, nor should we; indeed, the more traditional handcrafted products have, in many fields, developed their own market niche and their own marketable qualities. What we have to learn to do is to use energy more efficiently and – in some situations – to use much less.

5.2.1 Energy management

Over recent years there have been several studies which have shown that most businesses can save as much as 10% of their energy consumption simply by doing things differently. This might include reducing the thermostat, so that heating is just 2 or 3 degrees lower; a campaign to get staff to turn off equipment, lighting and heating when it is not in use; reducing the temperature of hot water by a few degrees. All these simple steps would reduce energy costs for the business, but they will only make an impact if the savings are measured; your finance department has a role to play here. Once the savings are measured, the money saved should then be reinvested in better energy technologies, more efficient lighting, draught-proofing, insulation and other simple measures which will help to save even more money which, in turn, can be reinvested.

One way to do this is to meter electricity consumption in specific areas or operations.

Case study: Heinz production lines

The food manufacturer H K Heinz set about sub-metering its production lines, and then gave its production managers the responsibility of identifying where energy savings could be made. The advantage of this approach is that it allows similar processes to be compared, differences to be identified, and solutions tried and shared. Solutions are also likely to be 'owned' by relevant staff, and are more likely to be effective.

Case study: The office block – 1

A local authority in north London, with a large 10-storey office block and a vast energy bill, asked for propoals to reduce its energy consumption. One suggestion was to incentivise staff by giving them 50% of any savings made, a system which could be implemented on a floor-by-floor basis. Although officers supported the idea, the councillors' reaction was summed up as 'They should not need an incentive to do this.' Nothing changed.

Case study: The office block – 2

A subsidiary of a bank with an eight-storey building in north London had major heating problems. The lower floors, nearer the boiler, were excessively hot, while the top floors were only just acceptably heated. The company had failed to put an efficient heating system in place – and then had failed to meter it on the different floors to find out what was happening.

The aim of energy management in your business should therefore be to do the same amount of work as before but by using less energy. The range of business activities which need to be examined in order to reduce energy consumption in your business are, of course, diverse but could include:

- **Heating**
- **Hot water**
- **Building fabric**
- **Compressed air**
- **Utility purchasing**

- **Lighting**
- **Cold water and cooling**
- **Electrical equipment**
- **Vehicles.**

For each of these elements, some suggested actions and details will be discussed in the next section of this chapter.

The overall concern about energy use for your business is the imperative to:

- **Maximise the efficiency** of all the equipment which uses energy
- **Investigate alternative sources** of energy other than fossil fuels and their suitability for your business
- **Research different suppliers** and the tariffs which would apply to your business
- **Monitor energy use** in specific areas.

5.2.2 Energy costs

In February 2002 the UK Government identified that the reduction of waste and control of energy consumption were the two priorities for environmental improvement in the UK. The focus on the reduction of energy use was further enhanced when the Government signed the Kyoto Protocol, which committed the UK to reducing CO_2 emissions by 12.5% below 1990 levels by the year 2010. In fact, the UK went beyond the Kyoto Protocol and set domestic targets of a 20% reduction.

In response to these agreements and objectives, the Government implemented the Climate Change package of measures, which included the Climate Change Levy (CCL); this introduced an additional cost for electricity, oil and gas usage. This additional cost was to be discounted against employers' National Insurance contribution. However, this discount was offered to all employers and not targeted specifically to fuel users. It was, therefore, not an integrated policy: employers paid lower NI contributions, but did not have to address the reduction of energy consumption.

Many businesses have thus not been making the level of savings they might have done if they had been given better incentives.

The current (2004) rates of the Climate Change Levy are:

- 0.43p/kWh for electricity
- 0.15p/kWh for gas
- 1.17p/kWh for coal
- 0.15p/kWh for oil
- 0.96p/kWh for LPG (liquefied petroleum gas)

It would not be surprising if the Climate Change Levy were to increase steadily over the next few years. The rationale for this is that it will require higher tax levels to bring about real changes, because current evidence suggests that the present level of CCL has produced little difference. The other reason for CCL increasing is that, just as most businesses treat energy costs as a 'hidden cost', they will treat the CCL as a 'hidden tax' – and it will remain hidden until it increases to a level which cannot be ignored.

The other pressure for increase in energy costs is the cost of the fuel itself. All the indications are that the low gas prices we enjoyed in the 1990s are over and they are going to rise steadily. This will automatically mean that all the other energy costs will rise.

Stop press!

As this book was about to go to press, in early December 2004, the UK Government announced that it was not going to meet its target of 20% reduction of 1990 CO_2 emission levels by 2010. Some observers suggested that we might struggle to meet the 12.5% target which is our international obligation. The implication of this is likely to be that, in order for this country to get 'back on track' for our CO_2 reduction targets, increasing energy costs are likely to be a feature.

It is, therefore, imperative that businesses address energy management in their organisations as soon as possible, otherwise their costs from energy use will become a serious burden for the company.

Case study: Shorter hours = less energy
A medium-sized manufacturing company of about 80 employees in north London has seen its energy consumption reduced considerably by moving production onto a four-day week. The factory section and the machinery in it works for nine and a half hours every four days. Because some of the machinery has considerable start-up energy requirements, and along with not needing to heat or cool the factory, the company has made considerable energy savings. It has also noticed that productivity has increased and staff morale has also become more positive. In addition, Fridays (when the factory is shut down) is used for machinery maintenance. Although the office section continues to work five days a week, the heating and lighting system for the offices is separate to the factory and can be kept running.

5.2.3 Energy and global warming

It is the burning of fossil fuels which is believed by many scientists to be contributing to global warming, and it is the emission of carbon dioxide from this fuel burning which is the major contributor to global warming. The amount emitted from different types of building is set out below.

Type of building	Lower emissions Kg CO_2/m^2	Higher emissions Kg CO_2/m^2
General manufacturing	90	125
Factory office	80	115
Light manufacturing	65	110
Storage and distribution	50	70

Burning fossil fuels emits not just carbon dioxide but also methane, nitrous oxides (often referred to as 'nox') and sulphur oxides (sox) which all contribute to atmospheric pollution as well as to global warming.

The emission of a range of gaseous pollutants becomes especially important when transport is concerned. Transport contributes to about 25% of the direct energy costs of a typical business, but in addition to this there are the costs associated with traffic congestion and the purchase and depreciation of new vehicles. The position is further exacerbated in built-up areas during hot and sunny weather, when the sunlight reacts with these pollutants to produce more hazardous chemicals including low-level ozone, which is a hazardous product. This then results in increased admissions to hospitals of people with respiratory problems. In some European cities, notably Athens and Milan, traffic has to be cut by half in the hot summer months, to prevent this dangerous pollution.

The move towards liquefied petroleum gas (LPG) as a fuel for vehicles would have advantages for carbon dioxide emissions. The amount of CO_2 emitted per unit of LPG is significantly less than for the same unit of petrol; this explains why vehicles using LPG are (currently) exempt from the congestion charge in London. Other alternative fuels include hydrogen, which is likely to become more available over the next few years, and their use is likely to increase – especially if other cities establish congestion charging zones with the same discounts or exemptions.

Case study: Diesel from waste
Oil3, a new company in north London, has purchased equipment from Germany which allows waste vegetable oil to be converted to biodiesel. At present, Oil3 is collecting waste oil from restaurants and catering outlets but is trying to expand. Apart from using a waste product, the diesel fumes are considerably reduced; less waste oil goes to sewers, and less fossil fuel is being burnt.

One option for generating power in businesses is to install a **combined heat and power system** (CHP), currently a favoured option by the UK Government, with grant supports often being available. Although CHP is gas-driven, its high level of efficiency contributes to releasing less CO_2.

There are other energy sources which do not contribute to global warming and some of these may be relevant to your business. An example could include businesses where wood is a waste material, such as furniture manufacturers, joiners, some building companies and timber companies. The waste wood could be a very useful source of energy and, if a waste-burning boiler is installed, could provide a very high percentage of the energy required by the factory. There are now several manufacturers of these boilers and the costs involved in this should be investigated if you are in this business sector and a cost/benefit analysis carried out.

These systems don't add to global warming, as the wood comes from trees recently felled – but which have grown by accumulating CO_2 from the atmosphere over a number of years. Burning wood waste is (simplistically) thus simply returning CO_2 to the atmosphere from which it recently came. Although the burning does produce some pollutants, modern boilers have effective filters fitted to minimise the amount released to the atmosphere.

5.2.4 Energy and the environment

Apart from the impact on global warming, we should also appreciate that energy consumption has an extensive and significant impact on the environment in general. Fossil fuels themselves impact on the environment at the point where they are extracted (whether from the ground or the sea bed); as they are transported to the refinery; during the refining process itself; and at the filling station.

Some of the alternative energy sources have similar impacts on the environment: the **coal tips** in northern England are proving very difficult to revegetate and they continue to pollute local rivers. **Nuclear power** stations, although not contributing to global warming, produce radioactive waste – and the power stations, when decommissioned, will have to be quarantined for centuries.

'Natural' sources of energy

Hydroelectric power requires the construction of a reservoir and changes to the flow patterns of rivers; they also require a large land space for flooding, allowing for the overspill of the hydro dam. **Wind generators** are causing increasing alarm in the UK, because of their impact on landscapes: they are typically sited along the ridge of hills, often in attractive areas; offshore sites are beginning to raise some concern about their impact on birds.

Solar power has been used on a small scale for many years, and the development and enhancement of photovoltaic cells allows an effective conversion of solar energy to electrical power. Of all sources of energy, this probably has the least impact upon the environment. The potential is quite amazing: in half an hour, enough of the sun's energy reaches the Earth's surface to meet the world's energy demand for a year.

Landfill gas is a potentially useful source of energy: pipes are set out within the landfill and they collect the gas before it can escape to the atmosphere. By burning this at an electricity generation plant, it provides the double benefit of reducing emissions of very harmful greenhouse gases while generating electricity (which would otherwise have had to be provided from other fuels). **Wave power**, **geothermal heat** and **biogas** from farms are, as yet, minor technologies which have yet to develop to a commercial scale.

In summary, there is no form of major energy generation which does not have an impact on the environment; our problem will be moving to a pattern of energy generation which meets our needs without significant environmental impact. The other option, and the best in the immediate future, is simply to reduce energy consumption.

5.3 Managing energy in your business

There are many publications which provide businesses with advice – sometimes very specifically addressed to particular industries or sectors – and help as to means of reducing energy consumption. Some of these are listed at the end of the chapter.

You need to be clear about how you pay your energy bills. Many companies occupy rented buildings where the utility costs for energy and water are included within the total rental costs; in these circumstances, no matter how little energy you use, your business rent will not change – so there is little incentive for your business to make savings, but you should discuss this with your landlord. However, if your company owns or leases your property, there are a series of steps you should take:

- **Make someone responsible**
- **Get the facts** – check meter readings in different areas of the operation
- **Compare performance with potential** – there are guidelines for energy consumption for most types of operation
- **Identify the specific improvements**
- **Get the finance staff involved**
- **Take an energy tour**
- **Find some external advice and help**
- **Establish a staff team**
- **Set an example**
- **Celebrate success.**

Let's look in more detail at these issues.

- **Make someone responsible.** Ideally, this should be an employee in a key position in the company, with the authority to obtain information and make changes. If this is just not practical, consider employing a consultant – but if you opt for this strategy you must be prepared to adopt changes and make savings in order to recoup the consultant's fees. Note that there are some consultants and energy providers who will give free advice on the basis of them receiving a proportion of the savings

- **Get the facts.** The easiest way is to regularly monitor your energy, gas, water and vehicle fuel bills. This will indicate the costs concerned, and most bills will also show the quantities consumed. Compare the monthly bills for the current year with those for previous years: this will indicate how consumption has changed – and also how it varies month by month. If it is possible, meter energy use in different areas of the business – remember the Heinz case study, in section 5.2.1.

■ **Compare performance with potential.** Set up an exercise over a three-week period to show by how much your business energy costs could be reduced. This can be done at any time of year; the period of November to March is usually best to show heating and lighting costs, but will probably not indicate savings that could be made by reducing air conditioning. Try the 3-week energy self-assessment audit, shown on the next page, to identify your potential savings.

Here are some general tips to help reduce consumption:

- Make the most of natural daylight, especially in warehouses and store areas where skylights are – or could be – fitted
- Limit exterior lighting to hours of darkness
- Clean light shades regularly: dirty shades greatly reduce lighting levels
- Turn down thermostats or switch of heating rather than open windows
- If you are leaving a building unoccupied, switch off all lights as well as the heating
- Use a timer system to automatically control the heating system, thus avoiding unnecessary heating outside work hours
- Switch off lights when not in use
- Switch off photocopiers if not required for a longer period of time. A photocopier left on overnight uses enough energy to produce 5,000 A4 copies
- Switch off your computers if you are not going to use them for an hour or more. Ensure monitors automatically go into 'sleep' mode if not used for a period of time
- Adjust the thermostat temperature to that which is most convenient for you to work in. On warm days, turn the thermostat down: just a 1°C reduction can reduce energy consumption. According to the Energy Office, heating costs rise by 8% for each 1°C of overheating.

Energy self-assessment audit

Week One
Day one:
Take a reading of the electricity or gas meter at the beginning of the first day of the week and note it below.

Day eight:
On the morning of the eighth day, take the reading on the electricity or gas meter and note that; the difference between the two readings is your energy consumption for a period of seven days.

> ***Week One readings***
> Meter reading on day one   (a)   [   ]
> Meter reading after seven days   (b)   [   ]
> Energy consumption in Week One (b-a)   [   ]

Week Two
Day eight:
Now start educating your employees with some good tips on energy reduction. Train them to follow these tips strictly from today.

During the week
Interact with the employees and see how they are performing. Remind them of these simple steps to reduce energy consumption. Print or buy posters of the guidelines shown earlier and post them on noticeboards in each department.

Week Three
Day fifteen
On the beginning of the first day of the third week, check your electricity or gas meter again and calculate the energy consumed during Week Two.

Day twenty-one
Check your electricity or gas meter once more, and calculate the energy consumed during Week Three.

> ***Week Three readings***
> Meter reading on day fifteen   (a)   [   ]
> Meter reading after seven days   (b)   [   ]
> Energy consumption in Week Three (b-a) [   ]
>
> Units of energy consumed in Week One   [   ]
> Units of energy consumed in Week Three   [   ]
> Reduction in energy consumption   [   ]
> Money saved   [   ]

5

At the end of Week Three, there should be a reduction in the consumption of energy unless there has been some excessive use of energy at some point during Week Two that was not used in Week One.

It may be possible that one week may be too short a period to educate and direct all the staff to follow all the energy-reduction tips.

> **Case study: Energy-saving potential**
> Middlesex University used this three-week energy reduction technique on one of its campuses. At the end of the second week, not much reduction was seen in the energy consumption. But at the end of the third week, a substantial drop in energy consumption was noticed, saving the university thousands of pounds.

- **Identify the specific improvements** you are going to make and set some targets - but recognise that you will not be able to achieve them all at once! It will probably take several years; each year you should tackle new tasks and reinforce the message to staff. In the first year or two tackle the easiest options first, the ones where you will see big changes and good savings. Also, tackle those that do not involve any investment – such as changing thermostat levels, staff actions, supplier and tariffs

- **Get the finance people involved.** Usually they are the section who pay the bills and can tell whether costs are increasing and decreasing. They are also the people who will be able to identify savings which could then be reinvested in further improvements. If energy use goes up, try to identify the reasons for this

- **Take an energy tour.** By walking around your site at different times of the day you will get some idea of where (and when, and why) maximum consumption is occurring and where there is any evidence of wastage. You may find it helpful to get a member of staff who is familiar with a particular area to accompany you and explain what you see. However, beware of staff who tell you something has to be like that because it is the easiest way, or because it has always been done that way: this is usually a good indication that there is potential for savings! During this tour, have your energy consumption figures available so that you can check on patterns of use.

You need to ask some key questions during this 'tour' about the different equipment in use; use the following chart as a guide.

Energy use	Type of wastage	Action needed	Action taken
Lighting In offices, lighting can account for about 50% of the energy consumption	• Inefficient lights • Staff not switching off lights when not needed • Over lit areas, such as corridors and stores	• Use energy-saving bulbs and 26mm fluorescent tubes • Posters, advice, persuasion, encouragement, incentives • Switch off or remove some strips • Install movement sensors	
Heating This is the other major contributor to energy consumption in offices and factories	• Overheating – recommended temperature is 19°C • Identify areas where heating can be reduced • Draughts from doors and windows • Heating on for too long and radiators cannot be individually controlled	• Check the temperature independently (thermostats are not a very good indicator) and discuss with staff • Identify areas where heating can be reduced • Reduce temperature where possible. • Fit door closers and draught-proofing seals • Check and vary timings month by month and fit individual thermostats on radiators	
Water Hot water is necessary but careless use costs lots of money	• Water is too hot • Taps are dripping • The amount of stored hot water exceeds requirements • Are all boilers and pipes well insulated?	• Reduce water temperature to 60°C but no lower • Repair and maintain • Check use level against amount stored • Insulate as needed	

Buildings Effective insulation can save money and make staff more comfortable, but adequate ventilation is also needed	• Are heated and unheated areas effectively separated? • Are roof areas well insulated? • Are outside doors and especially loading bay doors open for minimum time? • Too much space to be heated?	• Check on heat flow from hot to cold areas • Check and insulate • Check door mechanisms and fast closing shutter doors • Consider installing suspended ceilings
Electrical equipment Electricity is expensive; simple controls on electrical equipment can make big savings	• Are computers, printers etc switched off when not in use? • Is air-conditioned computer equipment in the coolest area and properly cooled? • Do motors have variable speed drives (VSDs) fitted? • Equipment has poor efficiency rating	• Train staff and install automatic shut down devices • Check and relocate and cool as little as necessary • Fit VSDs where appropriate • Select the most energy-efficient equipment when buying new
Boilers Poorly maintained boilers are a significant energy wastage	• Poorly maintained boilers • Boiler operates when not needed • Boiler is not the most efficient type • Boiler is too large for the requirements	• Check weekly, certainly monthly; service annually • Boiler *heating* turned off in summer, but hot water is still available • Consider installing a CHP system or a condensing boiler • Check boiler requirements

5

Compressed air Costs ten times more than electricity	• Leakage • Air produced is more than needed • Electrical equipment is an alternative • Air produced generally and not locally	• Check and repair • Provide only minimum pressure required • Research the options • Locally produced air can be tailored to local requirements	
Vehicles Can make up to 25% of company energy costs	• Over-large company cars and vehicles • Poor driving practices • Poor maintenance • Petrol engine vehicles	• Offer staff small-engined vehicles • Driver training • Regular servicing • Investigate alternative fuels	
Buying energy Businesses often do not have the tariff best suited to their needs	• Not maximising on cheap-rate periods. • Incorrect metering • Uncompetitive supplier • Not asking supplier to help you reduce energy consumption	• Check your tariff • Double-check meter readings • Compare suppliers against tariffs and your use pattern • Some suppliers will provide expert help	
Other Specific to your business			

- **Find some external advice and help.** Having tackled the easy steps, you will need to identify what the next improvements should be. Some of this will be very specific and may need detailed examination to identify the most beneficial to you. Much of this help is free (see below); alternatively, you can get 'paid' help on the basis of sharing the savings

- **Establish a staff team** to keep the process going and cascade the strategy through the whole company. Alongside this establish, and get Board approval for, an energy efficiency policy

- **Set an example.** Nothing demotivates staff more than to be asked to take initiatives such as described earlier but then see management not bothering

- **Celebrate success** – use your savings to provide incentives to staff by holding a celebration, or buy them all a gift. But only do this if there is improvement year on year.

5.3.1 The future

Such is the importance of energy management, both on a global scale and on an individual scale in your business (and home), that it will become more and more important to the national and your business economy over the next decade or so.

There are several steps you should consider:

- If your heating system is in need of renewal, consider replacing your old boiler with a combined heat and power (CHP) system. Apart from increased efficiency and lower CO_2 outputs, the UK Government is currently (2004) offering grants, tax breaks and loans to encourage businesses to install them

- If you are moving to new premises, whether new-build or refurbished, spend a lot of time addressing all of the energy consumption, insulation and generation options which are available. Although the initial capital cost will be greater, the payback will be fairly short. A good architect, sound advice and information from Government agencies or the Building Research Establishment (BRE) will be a starting point

- From 1 January 2005, companies in energy, steel, building materials (among others) will only be allowed to emit a certain level of CO_2. If they exceed their limit they will need to buy additional 'allowances' from companies which are below their limit. The European Emissions Trading Scheme (ETS) is likely to favour energy-efficient companies and those generating electricity from alternative (non-fossil) sources.

Alternative fuels will become increasingly common and less costly, though it is highly likely that the overall cost of energy will rise steadily in the coming years.

At present the UK Government is offering businesses a variety of grants and loans to invest in several different types of improved energy equipment – but these will not last for ever.

It is never too soon to start addressing – and reducing – the energy consumption in your company; there is lots of free help and advice available, some of which is available from the organisations listed below.

5.4 Sources of information

The Carbon Trust   Government-sponsored company assisting
                             businesses reduce carbon emissions and use
                             low-carbon technologies. Can provide free
                             audits, loans etc.
                             www.thecarbontrust.co.uk/carbontrust

Combined Heat and Power
                             Sound information and contacts.
                             www.chpa.co.uk

Conservation of energy   Promotes energy conservation.
                             www.ukace.org

The Department of Trade and Industry's Energy Group
                             Website has information about publications,
                             latest legislation, statistics, etc. about energy
                             www.dti.gov.uk/energy

Energy 21   Sustainable systems, energy and other items.
                             www.energy21.co.uk

Energy Efficiency Best Practice Programme
                             Government programme to help
                             organisations cut energy bills.
                             www.energy-efficiency.gov.uk

Energy Information Administration
                             US Government site with lots of information.
                             www.eia.doe.gov

European Renewable Energy Exchange
                             Promotes renewable energy; good sources of
                             information www.eurorex.com

Energy Saving Trust   Provides stimulus to energy saving in homes, businesses transport and much else.
www.est.org.uk

Energy Technology Support Unit
Centre of excellence for energy efficiency and alternative energy technology.
www.etsu.com

The National Energy Foundation
UK charity providing energy advice, accreditation, rating and related information.
www.natenergy.org.uk

Renewable Energy **magazine**
Interesting articles and product lists.
www.re-focus.net

Solar power   See the website of West Wales ECO Centre for some interesting facts, figures and factsheets.
www.ecocentre.org.uk/solar-electricity.html

Thames Energy   Promotes energy efficiency in buildings
www.lessenergy.co.uk

World Energy Efficiency Association
Links and information on energy efficiency and international reports.
www.weea.org

Water and air

6

Case study

A house-building company in Wales was prosecuted in 2004 and fined in excess of £2,000 for allowing suspended solids to wash off their site into a nearby river, causing pollution and contamination. At the hearing the Environment Agency stressed that it offers freely available advice about proper pollution prevention.

Environment Agency staff had earlier visited the site and required the company to build a protective bund; on a subsequent EA visit, the bund that had been constructed was found to be inadequate and leaking.

6.1   Overview

6.1.1 Water

Two environmental issues which are significant, but often overlooked, comprise the consumption and use of water and the emissions of different gases to the atmosphere. It is important to recognise that this issue encompasses not only the amount of water consumed, but also the quality of water that is used – and the quality that is returned to the river or reservoir. So far as most businesses are concerned, the cost of water usage is based upon the quantity of water which passes through their system, whether or not it is actively, and usefully, 'used'.

'Using' water implies that the water will be contaminated to a greater or lesser extent. The contamination may be from chemicals, such as detergents, cleaning chemicals or a wide range of processing agents, and can also arise through increasing the temperature of water where it is used as a coolant in various processes. In addition, contamination may arise through the use of the water to wash physical materials from equipment and products, resulting in a suspension of the solid particles within the water. Unless converted into steam or ice, water cannot be 'used up' in the sense that it will disappear (unlike the burning of coal or oil, for example) but it can have its quality reduced, with the result that it will become expensive to clean or simply not immediately available for use by other businesses.

Lowering the quality of water, which may result in it becoming unsuitable for further use, is also likely to adversely affect the environment. Contamination or pollution of water is a serious problem for invertebrates, fish and plants which live in the water; there is a knock-on effect on the bird population which feed on some of these plants and animals; there is also the risk of contaminants in the water reaching the human population.

Within the UK, the quality of water is monitored by the Environment Agency; companies who wish to discharge materials into water usually need consent from the Environment Agency in order to do so. However, there are occasional accidents and spillages which result in serious damage to river or reservoir waters. The duration and severity of such damage clearly depends on the nature of the pollutant. A major concern is that many pollutants arise out of new and different processes, and their impact on the environment is not always obvious or identifiable.

In many instances, water is used very freely in businesses and in homes. Many people consider water the same as air – free, or of insignificant cost: the number of hotels and restaurants in which taps are left running for most of the day is considerable, as is the even greater number of organisations with dripping taps or leaks. Water is no longer cheap: its costs are increasing and the real cost of treating water is also increasing.

For businesses it is important, both financially and environmentally, to ensure that:

■ Water is used carefully

■ Water leaves the company as clean as possible

■ All leakages are identified and repaired.

Although water is not completely free, the air we breath is. But, like water, air is subject to legislative control so that your business cannot just place whatever it wishes into the atmosphere. Businesses which normally emit gaseous material or dust into the atmosphere need to ensure that they have the proper permit to do so, which will depend on the nature of the material as well as the quantity.

6.1.2 Air

Air quality is also important, not just to many businesses for their processes, but to the health and welfare of all of us.

The quality and cleanliness of air is probably more critical to human health than water; bottled water is nowadays available at all supermarkets, shops and garages – but we have no similar alternative to 'fresh air'. What is also beyond dispute is that when the air quality is poor there is a rise in the hospitalisation of people with respiratory disorders. Although since the 1950s we have reduced the amount of *smoke* in the air there is still a significant amount of sulphur dioxide (often referred to as sox), nitrous oxides (referred to as nox), carbon monoxides, ozone and small particulate matter.

Sox, nox and other airborne pollutants are very dangerous which, in the UK, are only slowly being reduced. If you fly in the UK on a clear day and look over a city, a brown haze can clearly be seen: this is made up of the sox and nox gases. On hot sunny days in the summer, these gases, as well as the other pollutant gases, can interact and produce potentially dangerous conditions. Recent data from the Government shows that, in the hot summer of 2003, the number of days when such air pollution was moderate or worse rose significantly compared to previous years. If global climate change continues, with an increasing number of hotter summers, these condition are likely to increase (DEFRA National Statistics, 2004).

The quality of water and air in the UK is improving and pollution levels are reducing – but there is still a long way to go. As different chemicals are invented and released into the air or water, this poses ever-greater challenges to remediate them; it will continue to be important to monitor and control pollutants and minimise their levels – and thus minimise their effects. Particular concern is given to heavy industrial areas and around major roads and their junctions: this is where the level of pollutants can build up to unacceptable levels.

6.2 Essential environmental quality

6.2.1 Water legislation

Organisations generating trade effluent must apply for a 'consent to discharge', which is obtained from the appropriate sewage undertaker under the **Water Industry Act 1991**. The consent will detail the following information:

- The place to which the discharge consent relates

- The nature, origin, composition, temperature, volume and rate of the discharge, and the periods during which the discharge may be made

- Steps to be taken to minimise the polluting effects of the discharge

- Provision of facilities for sampling and monitoring

- Provision, maintenance and testing of meters for measuring or recording discharges

- Keeping of detailed records relating to the discharge and conditions attached to the consent

- Provision of information to the enforcing authority in respect of the discharge.

Foul drains carry contaminated water, trade effluent and domestic sewage to a treatment works. Discharges to the public foul sewer require authorisation by the sewerage undertaker and may be subject to the terms and conditions of a trade effluent consent. Process effluent (such as compressor or boiler blowdown, steam condensates, cooling water, pressure testing liquids, air conditioning water, vehicle and plant cleaning effluent, and yard washdown water) should all be directed to the foul drains.

The other major piece of legislation controlling water quality is the **Water Resources Act 1991**. This legislation controls the discharge of materials to 'controlled waters'. Controlled waters are rivers, lakes, ponds, the sea (out to 3km) and any groundwater. The prohibited materials include noxious, poisonous or toxic matter or solid waste. Any business wishing to discharge such material is required to get a consent from the Environment Agency; any discharge of material into a 'controlled water' whether deliberate, negligent or accidental is liable to prosecution.

6.2.2 Air pollution legislation

The **Clean Air Act** was introduced in the early 1950s. This followed the very bad smogs in London and other cities, and the sharp increase in admissions to hospital of people with respiratory problems, which resulted in many deaths.

The main target of this Act was to reduce smoke in the air resulting from burning coal and wood. The **Clean Air Act 1993** updates this legislation and, in addition, sets limits on sulphur dioxide emissions.

Air pollution is also controlled by the **Environmental Protection Act (EPA) 1990 (Part 1)**. This legislation sets up the Local Authority Air Pollution Control and identifies local authorities as the body responsible for implementing the air pollution legislation and controls.

> **Case study: The company and the olfactory record**
> In the late 1990s, CESMB was asked by a company to advise it on maintaining an 'olfactory record'. The company produces large screen-printed posters and similar products on a modern estate and neighbouring businesses had complained about the smells coming from the factory; these were mostly Volatile organic compounds and smelt like 'pear drops'. The local authority environmental health staff were called in and asked the screen-printing company to maintain an 'olfactory record', essentially a daily record of the frequency and strength of the 'smell'. The problem for the company was that since its staff all worked in the 'pear drops' smell all day, they had mostly lost their sensation to it. It was further compounded by the practice of mixing chemicals near the open doors. Further discussions with the company also revealed that its main competitors had moved to water-based chemicals – and were expanding as a result.

6.2.3 Integrated pollution prevention and control (IPPC)

Legislation is trying to pull together the control of air, water and land contamination, so that businesses are required to address these potential pollution aspects as a single entity rather than separately. Originally, IPPC applied to heavy and polluting industries, such as smelters and coke works, but it has steadily been extended so that it now covers a much larger range of industries, including printing and food manufacture.

IPPC applies strict limits regarding the release into water and air of a wide range of chemicals and requires organisations to monitor and apply best available technologies to reduce their discharges and emissions to stipulated levels. The legislation and its requirements are fairly complex, but the Environment Agency is very supportive of companies going through IPPC applications.

6.2.4 Pollution and the environment

Pollution has, possibly, the most damaging and long-lasting impact on habitats and the environment. There is also increasing evidence that pollution causes significant human health problems; in some cases there are proven links whereas in others evidence is not clear-cut.

The major problems are:

- **Killing of wildlife**: oils and many other chemicals which pollute the environment kill animals and plants, either directly or indirectly. Oil on the surface of water reduces oxygen levels in the water and much aquatic life dies. Other chemicals poison aquatic animals and plants, which may be eaten by other animals – which then accumulate more of the chemicals from their prey, often building up to a lethal dose

- **Habitat destruction:** pollutants can destroy habitats, usually by killing the plants that make up the habitat. The commonest example of this in rivers is eutrophication, which occurs when fertilisers flow into the river from farmland. The fertilisers encourage rapid algae growth, which then dies; as it decays, it uses the oxygen from the water – which then kills other life in the water

- **Food chain build-up:** this is a particular concern for food from the sea; molluscs (such as cockles) and crustaceans (such as shrimps) accumulate chemicals, as can fish. When eaten by humans, this can cause illness or disease. Since all our rivers flow into the sea, we need to be careful about what we put in our rivers

- **Human health:** respiratory problems are a significant problem for people living in areas where the air is of poor quality. It has long been known that air pollutants have killed off lichens and other plants, including trees, in areas of bad pollution. The extent to which people with asthma and other respiratory problems are affected by poor air quality is becoming increasingly clear

- **Leisure and pleasure:** polluted waters cannot be fished, are unattractive to walk or bathe in and make boating and other leisure activities unpleasant. Similar discomforts can occur from polluted air.

6.2.5 Surface water drainage

On any business site there should be two separate drainage systems:

- **Surface water drains:** these carry uncontaminated rainwater from roofs and clean yard areas to a watercourse or soakaway. Under some circumstances, treatment may be required before discharge. Surface water drainage discharges to a watercourse or to groundwater via a soakaway.

A discharge of waste water to the surface water drain will result in pollution. The formal consent of the Environment Agency is required for many discharges to controlled waters, including both direct discharges and discharges to soakaways. Such consents are normally granted subject to conditions being met; it is important to realise that they are not granted automatically.

Surface water drains should be identified and marked as such; one good idea is to paint a fish clearly on the drain cover. New *and existing* installations such as showers, sinks, laboratories, washdown areas and gullies should be connected to the foul drains – and not just the nearest drain because this is often the surface water drain. Oil separators can be used to prevent oil entering the water system

■ **Foul water drains:** these carry contaminated water, trade effluent and domestic sewage to a treatment works. This will normally require a consent from the sewerage authority (often the same as the local water company). This consent will depend on the type of material which is being discharged, and the quantity, and will usually stipulate the minimum flow rate which has to be maintained, the temperature, the composition of the effluent and the discharge point.

There are many legal cases each year which result from companies allowing, usually negligently, polluting materials to get into controlled waters (rivers etc) or effluent exceeding the consent to get into the foul drain. To demonstrate how easy it can be to break the law relating to water or air pollution, here are a few recent cases.

Case studies: Pollution

Wigton Cumbria – a company allowed a discharge of sulphides through a sewer grossly exceeding its permitted levels of discharge. **FINED**

River Marden – a national company had a diesel tank with a proper bund, but it was too small and in heavy rains 200 litres of diesel overflowed into the river. **FINED**

Abingdon – a company emptied some drums of bleach into the drains believing they were connected to the foul sewer. In fact they connected direct to the River Thames. **FINED**

Abstraction – a company over-abstracted by 65% from its borehole supply. It also failed to take daily meter readings of the quantities abstracted. **FINED**

Antifreeze – a forklift truck collided with a tank containing 5,000 litres of antifreeze, which leaked into a nearby brook. The company had previously been warned by the Environment Agency about the risks but no action had been taken. **FINED.**

6.3 The issues for your business

Clean water, like clean air, is a resource which, in the UK, is very much taken for granted. We all tend to assume that the water which runs out though our taps is clean and pure and this is almost invariably the case. However, water is a precious resource and the range of chemicals now being disposed of through the water system presents the water companies with problems in purifying the water.

Where businesses and other organisations are concerned, there are several issues which they may need to address when examining both the quality and quantity of water which they use.

Businesses can obtain water in two ways:

- Supplied by the local water company through the mains system. Normally this water is of drinkable quality and is thus able to be used for a very wide range of uses

- Water which is abstracted from rivers or from boreholes. Both of these sources provide water which may be of variable quality; the receiving organisation may therefore need to test and treat the water prior to use. However, this very much depends on the use to which the water is being put.

6.3.1 Water use

Water has a variety uses in businesses and some of these uses can be both excessive and highly polluting. Metering water use at each separate process *within* an organisation provides an effective means of identifying where heavy water use occurs within the company. Areas that may be measured include:

- Cooling water

- Process water

- Water used for cleaning

- Water used for sanitary purposes

- Steam raising

- Treating spills and leaks.

Processes that use large amounts of water can then be targeted for reduction measures. This has the dual benefit of increasing the efficiency of the process and reducing your company's water use – and thus costs.

6.3.2 Waste water costs

Waste water discharged to the sewer is usually charged per cubic metre, and paid monthly. The cost is currently set to rise at a rate greater than inflation. Water used in commercial processes becomes contaminated with soluble and insoluble materials and generates an effluent, which must be disposed of. Additional costs are incurred in disposal of this effluent: an effluent discharge consent details the volume, type and concentration levels of pollutant permitted in the discharge. The greater the volume of water and the higher the concentration of pollutants in the effluent, the more expensive the discharge cost will be, as the water company has to treat the effluent.

Minimising the concentration of pollutants that enter the effluent flow will greatly reduce your waste water disposal bill. Onsite treatment of the water to reduce pollutants, before the effluent is discharged, is a way to reduce effluent disposal costs. However, a cost/benefit analysis must be undertaken prior to this to assess the feasibility and benefits to your company.

Measuring and recording effluent concentration will ensure that you are meeting the requirements of the effluent discharge consent and avoid any fines for breaching the limit. Once effluent concentrations are known, ideas can be generated as to means of reducing the concentration and volume of effluent produced.

'Closing the loop', by reusing the water in addition to treating it, can lead to further cost savings and the feasibility of this should be investigated.

Trade effluent can be collected into a tank or vessel and then taken away for treatment by a specialised contractor, but the waste is still your responsibility under the Duty of Care legislation: you must ensure that it is treated properly and disposed of in accordance with environmental legislation. This is often a costly way of dealing with waste water, and treatment onsite may prove a cheaper alternative to this in the long term.

Effluent

Trade effluent includes any effluent discharged from trade premises, other than domestic sewage or surface water. It must be disposed of correctly to avoid pollution of the environment and to comply with environmental legislation. Trade effluent discharged into rivers and streams is toxic to aquatic life and can contribute to the problems of eutrophication.

Businesses discharging trade effluent to the public sewer must do so under a 'trade effluent consent', which details the quantity and quality of the effluent that the producer is allowed to discharge.

The sewerage undertaker charges the producer accordingly to recover the cost for the conveyance, treatment and disposal of the effluent. In turn, sewerage undertakers must gain consent to discharge the treated effluent to inland rivers or coastal waters.

Increasingly stringent water quality standards are being set at both EC and UK levels. Sewerage undertakers and any businesses discharging to surface water must meet strict discharge conditions.

A concern often raised is that reducing water usage will increase the concentration of contaminants in the effluent stream. It has been argued that, because disposal costs and legislative requirements are concentration based, there is no benefit from reducing water consumption.

This is incorrect on two counts:

■ Dilution with excess quantities of water in the effluent stream is not an efficient way of treating the contaminated effluent. Current best practice (and the approach required by the Environmental Protection Act 1990) is to minimise all emissions at source – not just dilute them down to an acceptable level

■ Levels of contaminant in the effluent steam must also be reduced.

Control of water pollution

Most pollution incidents are avoidable by careful planning of facilities and operational procedures, to reduce the risk of spillage. Most of the measures needed to prevent pollution cost very little, especially if they are included at the design stage. In contrast, the costs of cleaning up a pollution incident and compensating others can be very high. Pollution prevention measures may also offer substantial economic benefits, including:

■ Saving of expensive raw materials and products

■ Minimisation of site accidents

■ Reduction of the risk of prosecution for water pollution offences.

Introduction of pollution prevention measures is the first step but, to be effective, employees must understand why they are needed – and be trained in their use. At present, a magistrates court can impose a maximum fine of £20,000 on polluters; there is **no limit** on the level of fine that can be imposed by the Crown Court.

6.3.3 Common problems and remedies

Site drainage

Incorrectly connected effluent drains can cause severe pollution problems, which are often costly to remedy. It is essential to ensure that new or temporary facilities, such as sinks, showers, canteens, laboratories and washdown areas, are properly connected to the foul drain and not just the *nearest* drain, because this might be the surface water drain. It is your responsibility to know where the outlets drain to: ignorance is no defence in law.

All drainage systems should be maintained in working order. A programme of regular inspections should be established; gullies and sumps should be cleaned as required by suitably registered contractors. It is recommended that gullies, grids and manhole covers are colour-coded to aid identification using, for example, blue or green or a fish symbol for surface water and red for foul. Use notices where appropriate and keep a set of up-to-date drainage plans on site. Employees should be trained in the recognition and understanding of the codes and notices and their importance.

Deliveries

The handling of materials always involves a risk of spillages and accidents. It is therefore important to identify these risks so they can be minimised:

- Designated loading and unloading areas should be marked and isolated from the surface water drainage system

- Yard areas used for storage, handling and manufacturing should be roofed to reduce the volume of contaminated drainage for disposal and drained to the foul sewer

- Deliveries of oil and potentially hazardous materials should be supervised. If there is a spillage, it is essential that it is contained and reported immediately, and NOT be hosed down. Your company should ensure that delivery drivers have their own 'spill kit' and their employer has trained them in its correct use

- Automatic cut-off valves should be fitted to delivery pipes to prevent overfilling.

Envisaging the worst-case scenario

The attitude of most people to risks is that if it has not happened before, it will not happen in the future. Unfortunately this is not the case; 'unique' accidents, causing water pollution incidents, occur frequently, with the resultant costs and fines for the companies concerned.

Case study: The diesel tank

A company sited in the Lee Valley in Hertfordshire has a diesel tank for its lorries, sited next to the road leading up to the delivery and loading bays. The tank was 'believed' to be double-skinned but, as a precaution, CESMB advised that it should also protect the tank with a barrier. One month after the barrier was put in, a lorry reversed into the barrier. Since the company is less than 20 metres from the River Lee a potentially damaging pollution incident was averted.

Envisaging the worst-case scenario should therefore be undertaken with every liquid or gaseous storage or movement activity that takes place at your site. A useful approach to this is to complete an environmental risk assessment, a form for which can be found at the end of Chapter 13.

Storage and disposal of liquid waste

Liquid wastes, including solvents and oil, must be securely stored in bunded compounds prior to collection by a registered waste contractor. Under no circumstances should any waste liquids be discharged to the surface water system. Some liquid wastes may be discharged to the foul sewer via a designated facility, if an appropriate trade effluent consent is in place. It should also be remembered that the storage needs to be secure, and that the company have taken 'all reasonable steps' to protect the stored liquid waste against accidental and deliberate damage (such as vandalism or sabotage). Also remember that some solid waste, if stored in the open, could dissolve in the rain and wash away into a nearby river.

Case study: The salt store

A small company in Yorkshire kept a store of salt and grit in its yard for use in the winter. Unfortunately it was only covered with a tarpaulin and when it rained the run-off washed around the salt pile taking significant amounts down the drain and into the nearby river. Not only did this pollute the river and lead to the company being fined, but it was also wastage of a resource by the company.

Cleaning and degreasing

All cleaning activities (including the cleaning of equipment, yards, floors, containers and vehicles) can produce large volumes of polluted water. All cleaning agents are potentially polluting, even if manufacturers claim they are 'biodegradable' or acceptable for discharge to drains. Water containing detergents, disinfectants, degreasers or any other cleaning agent, including effluent arising from pressure or steam cleaners, must not enter surface water drains or soakaways and should be discharged to the foul water drain in compliance with the trade effluent consent.

Staff training

It is vitally important that your company ensures that all staff who handle – or might handle – liquid or gas materials know exactly what they *can, must* and *must not* do. Training needs to be accurate, detailed, rationalised and must spell out the consequences of not following the correct procedures. The training also needs to be followed up on a regular basis, and updated as necessary.

There is a wide variety of environmental training available from short, one-day, specialist conferences, to in-house training, through to a wide variety of degree-level qualifications. Some training is validated by particular organisations, notably the Institute of Environmental Management and Assessment, the Chartered Institute of Environmental Health and the Chartered Institution of Wastes Management.

One disadvantage of much environmental training is that it is very 'environment focused' and does not tend to include, or give credit for, the *business* aspect of the topics. One alternative to this is the work-based learning approach, which is a specialism within Middlesex University.

The best advice if you are interested in training is to contact your local university, your local business link or look in one of the environmental magazines listed under 'sources of information' at the end of Chapter 13. You can of course type in 'environmental training' into an Internet search engine, but do ensure that any specialist training is delivered by an organisation with the requisite skills.

6.3.4 What is the true cost of water?

The reasons for reducing water consumption have never been greater. Water supply costs have increased significantly in recent years and water companies predict further steep rises in the future. Water represents a significant cost: as a guide, companies with a turnover of £2 million spend between £20,000 and £40,000 annually on their water supply.

The true cost of water is often underestimated; it not only includes the purchase price and disposal costs, but also the following:

- Pumping costs: on your site in terms of electricity
- Maintenance costs associated with your company's pumps, pipework and flow meters
- Capital costs
- Water treatment onsite: prior to discharge
- Loss of valuable product in waste water: including raw material, product and cleaning materials.

The true cost of water may therefore be more than three times the amount you pay for supply and disposal!

6.3.5 Controlling air emissions

Emissions to the atmosphere are an important source of pollution for businesses to control. There are generally four scenarios which might result in releases of pollutants to air:

- **Continual slow release of gases from a regular normal process.** Since this is a regular and normal process, business managers should be aware of both the types of chemical and the amounts emitted. Filters should be fitted – and maintained – to ensure that such emissions are as low as reasonably practicable

- **Release of gases during maintenance or an equipment changeover.** These events may be unusual but also may result in a large emission. Such events should be carefully planned and all precautions put in place to minimise the risks

- **Releases arising from accident, negligence or vandalism.** These may be unusual but can involve large quantities of gas which can be harmful. Most instances result from poor training of the operators

- **Releases occurring from safety measures** caused by problems elsewhere in the plant.

There is a wide range of equipment in the form of filters, monitoring equipment, scrubbers and gas control equipment now available on the market which can help businesses identify and control their emissions.

As with most other environmental controls, it is most effective to address a series questions in order to minimise the risks of release of gas or liquids into the environment. The key questions, and the sequence in which they should be addressed, are:

- Can the process take place by using a different, less harmful, material?

- If a particular material has to be used, what is the minimum quantity that can be used and stored?

- What is the best available technology to provide a sealed process?

- If transfer or escape of gas cannot be avoided, what is the best available technology to prevent its escape?

- If material does escape, how is the quantity best controlled?

- If material does escape, how can it be treated to neutralise its impact on the environment?

- Have the relevant authorities been informed and legal consent been obtained?

6.4   Sources of information

Chartered Institute of Environmental Health

Access to a wide range of information and training relating to environmental health issues.
www.cieh.org

Chartered Institution of Wastes Management

Major professional body for waste and resource management, over 6,000 members; information on all aspects of waste management and training courses.
www.ciwm.co.uk

Chartered Institution of Water and Environmental Management

Offers free online service for anyone seeking a consultant, contractor, manufacturer or supplier in the environmental management sector. Range of direct or accredited education courses
www.ciwem.org.uk

Clean air   Look at the website of the National Society for Clean Air for lots of general information.
www.nsca.org.uk

Environment Agency   The Environment Agency's information page on water quality.
www.environment-agency.gov.uk/subjects/waterquality

Envirowise   The 'water' section on the webpage provides advice and information on saving water. You can also order free guides on 'water saving' and can arrange for a free water minimisation audit through this website.
www.envirowise.gov.uk

Institute of Environmental Management and Assessment

Access to a range of publications and training courses.
www.iema.net

Institute of Fisheries Management

International organisation dedicated to the advancement of fisheries management and offers a variety of training courses.
www.ifm.org.uk

Institute of Professional Soil Scientists

Can provide expertise on environmental protection and management; it accredits courses on soil sciences.
www.soilscientist.org

Royal Meteorological Society (RMetS)

Climatology, climate change and weather forecasting issues are at the heart of its operations. It also offer a range of training courses.
www.rmets.org

Thames Water

The 'Water Wise' section of this website provides valuable information and advice on savings water in your business.
www.thameswater.co.uk

Universities

Look at the website of your local university or training provider for accredited environmental related courses.

6

Design

7

Case study

Grant Instruments, near Cambridge, manufactures various precision scientific instruments such as scales and analysers. Until recently these were treated as equipment to be used until the end of their life and then disposed of. However, partly as a result of the WEEE Directive, the company is beginning to establish a 'repair and re-engineer' department. In turn, this has forced it to re-examine the *design* of its products, in order to make the new 'repair and re-engineer' process as straightforward as possible.

7.1 Overview

Environmental issues should be a concern for all products throughout their life. Originally, this was taken to mean 'from the cradle to the grave', but this concept was then updated when it was realised that the first step in developing a product was the *design phase*. Design which considered the environment was as important a criteria as other aspects such as safety, ease of use, aesthetics and functionality.

Legislation is also forcing changes to be considered to the design of products to allow them to be more easily re-engineered and recycled. Many new cars now claim to be 75% recyclable, a target which is likely to become law within the next few years. The best way to achieve this is to design that concept in, right from the drawing board. The concept of environmentally responsible design, or 'eco-design', is also important in contributing to the reduction of waste: products now need to be made in such a way that waste arising is minimised and, again, design plays an important part.

The concept of eco-design takes on board several other ideas and applies them to the design, use and reuse of a product; it treats the environment as of equal importance in the product design as the other concepts such as customer expectations, technical feasibility and cost control. It also considers the life of the product and all the direct and indirect environmental impacts that occur during the life of the product. However, it is also important that the function of the product is not impaired if an environmentally sounder alternative is developed. An example of this might be the WEEE Directive (see Chapter 2) which prohibits the use of lead in solders from 2005. If the replacement solders being developed require additional energy to be used, additional chemicals in replacing the lead or other requirements, it may be that the environmental impact of lead-free solders is actually greater than the lead solder. A headline saving should always be worked through to check 'whole-of-life' costings.

Design should, therefore, take on two other useful concepts:

- **Best Practicable Environmental Option (BPEO):** this concept sets up the idea that there are several options in the materials and manufacture process of a product and some of these may have better, or poorer, environmental impacts; the challenge is to fully investigate alternative options, to identify which alternative is most practicable, most cost-effective and the most environmentally sound

- **Best Available Technology Not Entailing Excessive Cost (BATNEEC):** this concept encourages the selection of technology which has lowest environmental impact within reasonable cost guidelines. This concept is applicable to design in that it should encourage designers to think about the balance between cost and environmental benefit for the technology being designed. It should also encourage the designer to consider the technology used in the manufacture of the product.

> **Case study: Designing in recycling**
> Syrris Ltd is a small company based in Royston, Herts, which designs and develops productivity tools for R&D chemists. It is a high-tech company, founded in 2001, with 20 highly trained and expert staff. Before starting a project guided by CESMB, Syrris made only limited consideration of environmental factors within its design specifications. It has now developed criteria within its R&D process manual which incorporate environmental issues into the design of its equipment, including the range and types of plastic, glass and metal in any new product. By reducing the range of these materials, re-engineering and recycling of the product is simplified, reducing overall product life cycle costs.

7.2 Eco-design: background

Life cycle assessment (LCA)

Life cycle assessment is a technique which has strong relevance to identifying the environmental impacts of a product or service. It looks at each stage of the production or service, from the extraction of raw material to the final stage of the product – whether that is disposal or recycling.

LCA involves:

- Identifying and quantifying energy and materials used, and the wastes discharged, at each stage of the life of the product

- Assessing the impact on the environment of those energy and material uses and waste releases

- Identifying ways to reduce the environmental impacts.

LCA has a number of applications which are, potentially, very useful to organisations, as it:

- Can assist in making decisions about the types of material to be used in the product, manufacture or service provided

- Allows the production and service processes to be examined in detail at each stage, and the particular environmental concerns identified

- Provides the basis for drafting an environmental policy

- Has links to ecolabelling (see section 8.2.7)

- Identifies the role of suppliers in the production process

- Gives clues about possible alternatives

- Acts as a comparison between different products and services
- Has a clear role in establishing the environmental effects of materials as part of an environmental management system
- Can lead to improved product design
- Has a marketing value.

It should be recognised that there are a number of problems with LCA, as there is no single agreed methodology; there are a number approaches and techniques, but it has been used in different ways by companies wanting to demonstrate the environmental advantages of their product over competitor products. The assessment of how the environment is affected is also subject to differing views, and the quantification of the impacts can require very considerable expertise. The current tendency is to ask an independent assessor to carry out, or at least verify, the LCA.

Case study: China or plastic?

In an attempt to reduce staff costs, companies have moved towards automatic vending machines and water cooler fountains in canteens and restaurants, and the china cup or mug has consequently become less common. A few years ago, a study looked at the environmental impacts of the plastic mug compared to the china mug and concluded that if a china mug could be used over 300 times it was generally more beneficial to the environment. This assessment is qualified by several conditions: the temperature of the washing water, the detergent used, the drying method used, the fate of the plastic mugs post-use, and the type and quantity of plastic used to make the mug.

A very simplified example of how an LCA could be applied to a product is shown, for a paper clip, overleaf.

In the whole life cycle, the amount of energy used, the different forms of that energy, the level of emissions to air, discharges to water and land contamination need to be identified and quantified where possible.

Once the outline scheme of a life cycle has been assessed, as in the paper clip example, that will be sufficient to give a fairly accurate assessment of the environmental impacts. However, in order to be definitive it is necessary to quantify the impacts on the environment. Alternative products and services can then be compared.

Simplified LCA diagram for a paperclip

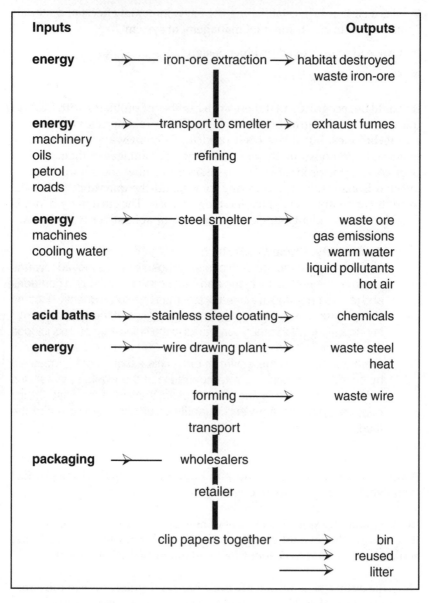

There are several alternatives to using paper clips. Staples are an obvious example: they use less metal, but are definitely a single-use item. An alternative is a staple-less stapler, which works by cutting and interlocking the page corners. A further alternative could be a plastic folder; these are more likely to be reused than a paper clip and at the end of their life can be incinerated to provide energy.

The technique of life cycle assessment is complex, and requires detailed analysis. In some instances they may result in no clear evidence in favour of one product or service or another. In other cases, the balance between alternative products will be qualified by different conditions.

The whole process of design, if it is to consider the environment properly, has therefore to include the life of the product, and all the different aspects involved, from the first concept of the product until it reaches the different alternatives for its post-consumer use.

7.3 Eco-design: business considerations

Guidelines for eco-design

It is often very straightforward to consider the environmental issues associated with a product, simply by paying attention to some well-known environmental ideas and concepts:

- **Design life cycles not products:** a product is the 'mid point' in the life cycle of a range of materials which can be brought together to perform a function. The designer should consider all the different stages in the life cycle of a product and select the options which, on balance, have the least environmental impact. This implies that the design should take account of the materials used, the energy involved in both production and use, and how the product can be re-engineered or recycled

- **Maximise product life:** products which have longer lives are generally more environmentally sound, because they are spreading the use of resources and production processes over a lengthy usage, and thus minimising the waste. Durability is an important factor for designers to consider; this is not just about designing something which is hardwearing, robust and sturdy but also equipment which can easily be repaired, upgraded or re-engineered. Most people discard products not because they are broken or become inadequate for the job but because they got bored with them, or because the cost of repair was prohibitive due to its complexity and resultant labour charges.

  Although this approach is not immediately to the benefit of manufacturers of new products, these manufacturers need to appreciate these changes and move into providing a repair and re-engineering service

- **Natural materials are not always better:** it is a common belief that 'natural' materials are more environmentally friendly than 'artificial' or man-made materials. Production of 1kg of wood causes fewer emissions than the production of 1kg of plastic – but you need to consider losses occurring when it is sawn and worked to shape, the energy needed to dry it and the paint to preserve the wood.

A good example of this would be plastic fence posts: it is now possible to buy fence posts that look exactly like wood but are made from recycled plastic. They are sturdy, durable and do not rot. Wooden posts will require rot-proofing treatment which takes energy and chemicals, ongoing treatment and, at the end of their life will, at best, be incinerated

■ **Remember the energy:** energy consumption is often overlooked at both the manufacturing stage of a product and also in the use stage of a product. For some products, such as cars, the energy consumed in their production far exceeds the energy they use in their lifetime; with other products, such as light bulbs, it is the other way round. Remember, too, that most plastic is manufactured from oil and is therefore just another form of 'locked-up energy'. As the pressure on businesses to reduce energy consumption increases, there will be more interest in energy-efficient manufacturing processes and energy-efficient equipment

■ **Design services not products:** virtually every home and organisation in the UK has a fridge and an oven; most homes have a washing machine. The question to ask is whether people want to own the item for its own sake – or whether what they want is a piece of equipment which will keep their food cooled, wash their clothes and so on. If this equipment is serviced on a regular basis and renewed by a more efficient fridge or washing machine and the old equipment is re-engineered before being leased to another customer, this would have a positive environmental benefit

■ **Rationalise material use:** this guideline is partly about minimising material use and also about being uniform in regard to the materials you do use. Using less material obviously makes environmental and economic sense, and computer-aided design systems optimise this. Consider trying to keep the range of materials in a product as similar as possible, as this makes recycling and repair much easier: if a product has ten different materials, it is clearly harder to dismantle and segregate for recycling than one with only six different materials. It should also be remembered that less material means less weight and this reduces transport costs. Pay attention to making your product recyclable and as easy to repair or re-engineer as possible. Legislation will require this, for many products, over the next few years

■ **Use recycled materials:** consider the use of recycled materials wherever possible, or materials which have been made from waste products. A good example of this is paper; many business ask for their literature and papers to be printed on recycled paper, but there is now a wide range of papers manufactured from maize waste and other wastes. These are known as environmental papers; speak to your printers about them and compare the costs and quality

- **Design in recyclability and re-engineering**: most products could be recycled – but few will. Only products that are disassembled easily and have a high enough yield will be chosen for recycling. The new WEEE Directive is forcing this to happen with electrical and electronic goods and we can expect this to cover other products in due course. Some companies have taken considerable steps in this direction: Rank Xerox re-engineer all their photocopiers rather than make new ones, and re-engineered printers for computers are easy to purchase – and significantly cheaper than brand-new printers.

> **Case study: Shades-Technics**
> This is a small company in Hertford that manufactures toilet cubicles for coaches. In order to make their hot water boiler more serviceable and lengthen its life span, they redesigned the heating element so that it was wrapped around the *outside* of the cylinder rather than the normal element *inserted* at the top. They accompanied this with repair instructions, which meant that replacing the elements was simple, straightforward and could be accomplished by mechanics within the coach company – rather than replacing the whole tank unit and requiring a plumber to do the work. Apart from being more efficient, the new design also reduces waste.

- **Question, question, question:** the most common reason for doing things in certain ways is *'That's the way we have always done it'* or *'We tried other ways or products and they do not work.'*

  In most circumstances these expressions cover up an unwillingness to change or, worse still, a reluctance to investigate other approaches properly. Part of the problem for many companies is that the people involved in the product or service are too close to the operation: it really needs someone to stand back and ask questions. One way round this is to empower staff from a different area of the company to question and challenge the way another department carries out its work. By way of example, one company produced a food packaging designed to keep the contents fresh for 18 months; after critical internal questioning it was discovered that its products were almost invariably consumed within three months. This realisation allowed for completely different packaging solutions

- **Use imagination and research – and communicate**: as environmental knowledge, awareness and materials become more common, it becomes much easier to develop existing products, or design new products which have much better environmental characteristics. It requires research and investigation into alternatives and should encourage businesses to involve a relevant environmental expert to discuss and advise on different options. Having taken these options, the next important step to take is to advise your customers of the changes and the benefits to them.

7.4 Sources of information

Centre for Design at RMIT

Melbourne's RMIT University. The Centre
develops new design tools and processes
including greener products.
www.cfd.rmit.edu.au

Eco-design

For links to many eco-design sites, visit:
www.greenmap.com/home/ecolinks.html

Furniture design

Canadian site with links to many eco-design
topics.
www.valuecreatedreview.com

Impacts

Cambridge University Engineering Design
Centre – some work on eco-burden of
different materials.
www-edc.eng.cam.ac.uk/technology/

The Institution of Agricultural Engineers

Professional body for those in agricultural
and allied landbased industries, including
forestry, amenity, renewable energy, and the
environment.
http://www.iagre.org/

The Institution of Chemical Engineers

Engineering for sustainable development
means providing for human needs without
compromising the ability of future
generations to meet their needs. IChemE has a
set of indicators to measure sustainability
performance of an operating unit.
http://www.icheme.org/

Publications

Visit the site of the publishers of *The Eco-
Design Handbook – a Complete Sourcebook for
Home and Office.* Enter 'eco-design' in the
search field on the home page of the website.
www.thameshudson.co.uk
Also, enter 'books on eco-design' into an
Internet search engine for a wide range of
other titles.

Sustainable design

Training, workshops, consultancy in product
and service development.
www.cfsd.org.uk

Purchasing and supply

8

Case study

Middlesex University has, over several years, been implementing a green supply chain policy. Operating through its Strategic Purchasing Unit, the university has been preferentially selecting *supplies* with better environmental properties and is now beginning to identify *suppliers* with better environmental performance.

It is, however, trying to do this in a collaborative way, and is offering its suppliers the opportunity to benefit from expertise at the university to help them improve their environmental performance. In the last two years Middlesex University has begun to develop its environmental purchasing into the wider issue of *sustainability*, thus taking account of financial and social issues as well.

8.1 Overview

As society and the provision of goods and services become more complex, so the sources and routes through which these goods are supplied become more extensive and complicated. It is, at present, extremely difficult to clearly identify all the companies and processes which lead from the raw materials to a final product.

For many products the original source may be some distant country where the purchaser doesn't know how the raw material is produced; nor is it aware of the associated activities with that raw material. This applies not only to the environmental qualities of a product, but also to social and community aspects: the use of child labour, or poor health and safety practices in factories in developing countries, which may be difficult to identify.

One early example of an attempt to set a standard for the provision of raw materials was the Forestry Stewardship Council. This was established to accredit timber supplies originating from forests which are managed sustainably. Originally established to try to control the use of tropical hardwoods, the scheme has extended to cover timber from forests in many parts of the world. However, it is important to recognise that the range and variety of products available for retail or wholesale far exceeds the number of schemes which can give assurance about the environmental and social background to the product.

The problem of purchasing environmentally sound products becomes compounded when equipment is purchased which is made up of a wide variety of complex materials and smaller components. A further problem is that in the construction of the equipment, the components may arrive from many different sources, involving their own transport and packaging issues. It is therefore extremely difficult for any purchaser of a complex piece of equipment to be assured of the soundness of each component and they are thus reliant upon information from the manufacturer or importer who, in turn, may be reliant on information provided by other companies further down the supply chain.

The increase in concern about purchasing of environmentally sound products and equipment has been driven, in part, by the increasing desire of major companies and organisations to follow and implement environmental management systems (see Chapter 11). A major aspect of these systems is to establish mechanisms to ensure that their purchases are as environmentally sound as reasonably practicable.

The supply of environmentally sound products and services should follow many of the same principles as set out in this chapter for purchasing; indeed, major customers are now requiring suppliers of goods and services to demonstrate positive environmental policies and practices. Suppliers who can develop and demonstrate their environmental credentials may be able to gain a significant competitive advantage over their competitors.

Purchasing and supply issues should not simply be concerned with knowing about the origin of products and equipment; they should also be concerned with establishing a collaborative arrangement with suppliers such that packaging may be returned and reused, and that new, more environmentally sound, materials can be developed. It is just as important for suppliers to develop this collaborative arrangement as it is for purchasers – both can be mutually supportive.

8.2 Environmental purchasing: the principles

8.2.1 The *Green Guide for Buyers*

A few years ago, the then Department for Environment, Transport and the Regions (DETR) developed a simple guide for buyers, addressing some of the reasons for buying environmentally sound products or services. These reasons are still valid.

- **Achieve best value for money** – taking account of whole-of-life costs can save money, not only on running costs but in many indirect ways

- **Fulfil the Government's commitment** to put concern for the environment at the heart of policy making

- **Withstand increased public scrutiny**

- **Meet international obligations.** The EU treaty commits the UK to integrate environmental protection into our policies. The Rio declaration requires us to reduce and eliminate unsustainable patterns of production and consumption

- **Stimulate the market** for green technologies, to provide technical solutions to our environmental problems

- **Improve – and maintain – our standard of living.** If we deplete our natural resources, insufficient will remain to meet future needs; prices will rise and standards of living will fall unless substitutes can be found

- **Improve health and the environment.** Efficiency reduces waste, and leads to a reduction in air, water and land pollution, and fewer problems such as global warming, acid rain and vehicle emissions

- **Save money** – avoid the need to pay for:
  - resources which are turned into pollutants
  - the cost of cleaning them up
  - the cost to our health and welfare systems arising from increases in illness caused by pollution.

(Source: - DETR: *Green Guide for Buyers, Part 1*)

Although environmental issues are an important part of supply chain management, they are only part of a wider approach which encompasses issues such as quality management, health and safety issues, equal opportunity criteria and, for overseas suppliers, the use of child labour and safe working environments. However, the information in this section will focus on environmental issues in the supply chain and help develop the approach sometimes referred to as 'greening the supply chain'.

8.2.2 What is supply chain management?

Supply chain management (SCM) can be defined as the flow of materials, parts, assemblies, information, ideas and people. Its aim is to minimise the costs and non-value-adding activities associated with each stage of the chain and at the same time increase the value-added, with a primary focus on the end user.

Supply chain management involves:

- **Supplier management**
- **Purchasing**
- **Material management**
- **Production scheduling**
- **Facilities planning**
- **Logistics**
- **Customer service.**

It is important to recognise that companies are usually both customers and suppliers: a firm that manufactures goods for its customer is also a customer to its own suppliers.

8.2.3 Whole-life costs

Whole-life costs is going to become an increasingly important technique as the buy/use/throwaway approach is replaced by the buy/use/repair /re-engineer/recycle strategy. Invariably the major consideration when making a purchase is the initial capital cost of the goods or equipment.

However, as energy costs increase, as waste disposal costs increase and modular repair strategies become more common, the capital cost may become less significant and the overall running, depreciation, disposal and maintenance costs will become more significant when considering which product to purchase.

When it comes to assessing the whole-life costs of a purchase, there are important elements which need to be considered.

These are:

■ **Direct running costs:** the resources, such as energy, used by the product or service over its lifetime

■ **Indirect costs:** less energy-efficient electrical equipment will turn electricity into excess heat, which in turn heats up the local environment and causes extra loading on cooling plants such as air conditioning. This can then be seen as an addition to the electricity bill

■ **Administrative costs:** when faced with a choice between a cheap (but relatively hazardous) product and a more expensive (but less harmful) option, it should be remembered that the hazardous option would have extra administrative costs in the form of COSHH regulations and the time that staff would have to spend on complying with these, not counting the potential cost of fines if regulations are breached

■ **'Spend to save' measures:** invest in higher levels of insulation within a building, so that the money can be recouped through the resulting lower heating bills over the building's lifetime

■ **Recyclability /refurbishment:** by buying recycled or refurbished materials, such as toner cartridges, you could be creating a market for your own waste and achieving savings by not having to dispose of it

■ **Cost of disposal:** by paying a premium at the outset, you can reduce waste or subsequent disposal costs: You can do this by choosing a product which is more durable, reusable and recyclable, or which includes disposal costs or which is free of hazardous materials requiring its disposal in a special way.

8.2.4 Benefits of implementing environmental supply chain management

Whether or not your company is involved in environmental supply chain management, it may face losses or gains. Managers actively involved in environmental supply chain management may benefit from the following:

■ **Advantageous position in respect of upcoming environmental legislation:** by being aware of upcoming environmental legislation, companies can avoid high-risk suppliers and invest in newer and cleaner technologies or products. Similarly, by encouraging suppliers staying ahead of legislative demands, they will be able to offer competitive products and/or a price advantage.

■ **Compliance with environmental legislation:** it is possible that your company can be held liable for practices you thought you were not responsible for. For example, the Duty of Care establishes that you keep records of all waste transfers. Transferring your waste to an unlicensed carrier may lead to *your* company facing criminal charges.

Case study: Removing COSHH

The replacement of a hazardous material with a more benign substance reduces administration, since COSHH Hazard Sheets are no longer required. The item can also be treated as general waste, removing the need for separation and the higher costs of using a hazardous waste contractor. This reduces your liability under the Duty of Care, by minimising the amount of waste produced and the risk of using hazardous material.

■ **Security of supply:** in order to secure a constant flow of supply, it is necessary to know if suppliers will be able to meet ongoing demand. Knowing your suppliers' corporate environmental performance is essential to be able to know how to choose the right supplier.

A supplier with a high environmental risk factor (a provider of hazardous material, for example) poses a potential risk to your company. If the supplier is prosecuted due to its environmental performance, your company may lose its primary source of supply and therefore incur significant financial losses

■ **Cost saving:** working with suppliers on minimising your waste or energy consumption can help you to obtain great savings. Environmental supply chain management avoids the need to pay for:
- resources which are turned into pollutants
- the cost of cleaning them up
- the cost to our health and welfare system arising from increases in illnesses caused by pollution

■ **Foster innovation:** by exchanging knowledge and technology with your suppliers, your business can gain competitive advantage by developing new products and services; by stimulating the market for green technologies, you can provide technical solutions to your environmental problems

■ **Improving communications:** it is essential that information flows up and down the supply chain, thus allowing companies to determine customers' needs and suppliers' capabilities. By working in partnership, customers and suppliers may find ways of saving costs

■ **Credibility:** if your company makes environmental claims, or has an environmental policy but any of its suppliers is prosecuted or highlighted in the media, the knock-on effects could damage your environmental and business credibility.

8.2.5 What if you are the supplier?

The above topics apply to any *purchasing* company, but the mirror image of each issue can also be applied to the *supply* side: as a supplier, you should be able to discuss new legislation, development issues and innovation.

Advantages of making environmental demands on suppliers:

- Identifying the effect your suppliers have on your environmental performance

- Potential to find and evaluate the right suppliers

- Possibility of establishing a dialogue, leading to an exchange of technology and knowledge

- Being seen as an 'environmental champion'

- Improving your overall business performance.

Advantages of receiving environmental demands from customers:

- Opportunity to understand better your company's processes

- Identifying ineffective production and distribution processes

- Identifying potential to get into new markets

- Establishing better relationship with customers

- Developing new technologies

- Being able to distribute the message to second-tier suppliers.

Risks

A manager who does not consider environmental issues will face the following risks:

- **Risk of prosecution:** any non-compliance with relevant legislation is likely to lead to fines – or worse. Prison sentences are not unheard of for non-compliance. If suppliers are having problems with compliance, then they could be passing these problems along the chain to customers

- **Bought-in liability:** customers must be confident that the goods which they buy and insert into their own processes will not cause pollution once they are in use. This is related to the Duty of Care principle (any company that produces, holds or is concerned with controlled waste is responsible for the safe passage downstream through the supply chain). For example, if your company employs contract cleaners, your company may be exposed to Duty of Care requirements if they (the cleaners) dispose of hazardous wastes

- **Loss of supply:** as scientific knowledge regarding environmental issues develops, environmental legislation will adapt to reflect this change – and this may restrict the availability of certain items. It is therefore necessary to be aware of upcoming environmental legislation and to be aware of alternative products and materials which may be substituted. This is where BPEO (Best Practicable Environmental Option – see Chapter 7 and section 8.3.1) comes in useful

■ **Loss of competitive positioning:** companies that cannot respond to their customers' environmental demands face the risk of losing competitive advantage. Developing an environmental purchasing policy is not about buying green goods; it is about working to minimise a growing strategic business concern, reducing costs and improving added value. As previously mentioned, one of the knock-on effects of the WEEE Directive is that lead in solder will shortly be illegal: this is causing manufacturers of items such as printed-circuit boards (PCBs) to look to alternative materials.

8.2.6 Building the environment into purchasing decisions

Here are just two examples of issues to consider when making purchasing decisions.

Green procurement of cleaning services and products

Actions:

■ Specify that products should be readily biodegradable: require, for example, that they break down within three to five days of use into harmless substances. Care should be taken when purchasing products that advertise that they are biodegradable: this statement is meaningless without a time span being assigned to it, as virtually everything is biodegradable over a sufficiently long time

■ Specify that cleaning products have low levels of biological oxygen demand (BOD) and chemical oxygen demand (COD). This is because most chemical cleaning products are discharged into the sewerage system after use, and those that have a high BOD and COD will have an adverse effect on freshwater flora and fauna

■ Consider the transport and delivery of chemicals (like cleaning products) in concentrate form, with dilution at the place of usage

■ Specify cleaning and treatment agents that are plant- or water-based and low in solvents. Cleaning products containing solvents give off volatile organic compounds (VOCs) which, in excess of specific levels, are harmful to human health and work to produce ground-level ozone

■ Specify that no abrasive chemicals should be used to clean timber in furniture, fittings or joinery

■ Specify that cleaning products must not contain ozone-depleting substances and ensure that there are adequate provisions for the scrutiny of materials used by contractors

■ Specify that the contractor uses, where possible, multipurpose cleaners, pump sprays instead of aerosols and phosphate-free detergents. Given optimum conditions, high levels of nitrate in freshwater systems cause rapid growth in algae which remove oxygen from the water when they die

- Specify that the successful contractor must conform to your environmental policies and ensure that any resultant waste is disposed of in the appropriate manner, that is, in a way that will not cause any environmental harm

- Specify, where there are viable alternatives, that chlorine-based bleaches and disinfectants are not used. This is because chlorine can form toxic chemicals as it breaks down.

Green procurement of paper

Research has shown that making paper from recycled fibres can use 70% less energy than from virgin fibres. Environmentally sound paper does not have to be recycled; there are currently many papers on the market which are made from maize or other vegetable wastes. The book you are now reading has been printed on 100% waste materials. The benefit of using environmentally sound paper is that it can maximise the use of a material before it is finally disposed of, and also that it is helping to protect natural resources. Apart from the use of particular raw material and energy, the other part of the paper-making process to be concerned with is the use of chemicals, including bleaches within the process.

Actions:

- Aim to use the maximum percentage of recycled content (post-consumer waste) while ensuring that it is suitable for the use intended and value for money

- Be aware of the respective differences between pre- and post-consumer waste recycled paper. Pre-consumer waste recycled paper contains materials and waste from the manufacture of virgin paper. These have always had a value for the manufacturer and consequently have always been collected. By purchasing paper with a high pre-consumer waste content you are benefiting the environment less than you would by purchasing paper with a high post-consumer waste content, as this contains fibres and other materials and would otherwise have been disposed of to landfill

- Specify that any paper bought must be manufactured without the use of chlorine as a bleaching agent. Less environmentally harmful alternatives do exist, in the form of oxygen, hydrogen or sodium peroxide

- Specify that the recycled paper should not be made using optical brighteners

- Consider purchasing paper that has been assigned an ecolabel (see next page) or equivalent based on the recycled content and source of its constituent fibres. The 'Blue Angel' is a German standard awarded to recycled papers that are made from 100% waste paper, 51% of which is low or medium grade

- Specify that the paper must be manufactured using water-based varnishes

- Specify that all contractors and suppliers must submit reports and all other written material on recycled paper and that these, along with any published or printed material specific to the contract, must be bound using water-based adhesives.

8.2.7 The ecolabel

For about the past eight years the European Union has been trying to spread the idea of a label which indicates that the goods to which it is attached conform to good environmental standards. Some countries in Europe have already developed their own labelling schemes for environmentally sound goods, with the Blue Angel scheme in Germany and the Nordic Swan in Norway.

In the UK we have generally not developed this approach, with the notable exception of the previously mentioned Forestry Stewardship Council, which has developed a scheme indicating that the wood or products from it have come from sustainably managed forests.

Within the EU, there are several hundred products listed as having gained an ecolabel – but only two of these have any connection with the UK.

There are arguments both for and against such labelling schemes; in the end, however, it is important to look behind the information and identify what the environmental characteristics of the product are, what the label *really* signifies – and how it has been awarded.

8.3 The supply chain and your business

8.3.1 Principles of environmentally sound purchasing

It would be very difficult to set out specific environmental issues concerned with every piece of equipment and material because the nature, manufacturing process, usage, number and type of components and style of items and materials are rapidly and continually changing.   Two examples of issues to consider have been provided in 8.2.6.

When researching into the purchase, or assessing your suppliers, there is one guiding principle that should be influencing your decision. This is the Best Practicable Environmental Option (BPEO). This principle, along with Best Available Techniques Not Entailing Excessive Cost (BATNEEC), was specifically mentioned in the Environmental Protection Act 1990 and is now considered an underpinning factor for the majority of UK environmental legislation.

The BPEO procedure establishes, for a given set of objectives (in this case the concept of best value), the option that provides the most benefit (or least damage) to the environment as a whole – at acceptable cost – in the long term as well as in the short term. This puts the emphasis on you to use this chapter and the methods advocated within it (the principles of environmentally sound purchasing and associated degrees of environmental and profile risk) to determine the BPEO for that specific purchase.

Below we have tried to set out some general principles which should be applied. Later in the chapter you will find a questionnaire setting out how these principles can be set out and used.

- **Reduction of the amount of material purchased:** purchase only the amount that is required. When preparing publicity materials, calculate carefully how much will be needed and stick to this amount; printers frequently try to persuade clients to buy more on the basis that it will be cheaper than getting reprints. Buying only the quantity required will also save money on waste removal costs (see Chapter 3)

- **Purchase reusable equipment:** the purchase of plastic or metal boxes which can carry goods and which can be used again and again

- **Select re-engineered equipment:** more and more equipment, particularly electronic and electrical equipment, is being re-engineered. The other side of this is to ensure that equipment at the end of its life should be sent for re-engineering, repair or reuse. Photocopiers, computers, and similar items are good examples of this

- **Recyclability:** can the product be recycled – and how easy is it to collect for recycling? Is the product designed to be recycled – and is the product itself recycled? Many businesses have drink machines which supply drinks in plastic cups; an organisation called 'Save-a-cup' can collect these and will turn the plastic into other goods.

The above are some general principles which also relate to waste reduction. Others questions to consider include:

- **Sourcing:** where have the materials come from, have they come from a renewable resource, such as a forest (if so, is that source certificated as being managed sustainably?) or is the material from a non-renewable source, such as fossil fuel? Are the materials transported over long distances, or are there local alternatives? (By way of example, one London borough realised that several of its contracts, especially for building works, had been let to companies up to 50 miles away. Not only was this contributing, albeit in a small way, to traffic congestion in the borough but it was not providing job opportunities for their residents.) One of the other major changes in the past few years has been the increase in 'fair trade' products and this is another aspect that businesses could look at to improve their practices and performance

- **Type:** what are the alternative materials, and are their effects on the environment greater or less than the item in question? What is the cost differential, and does this outweigh the environmental benefits? For example, paper can either be virgin paper manufactured from trees, recycled, or paper made from waste materials – including maize waste. Your printers should be able to advise you of the different types and you can decide which is most suited to the needs that you have

- **Manufacture:** what energy is used in the production of the materials or equipment? Are there more energy-efficiently produced materials? What is the type and extent of pollution associated with the manufacture of the product? For example, desks can be made of wood, plastic or metal and may involve the use of glues, solvents, colourants and paints, all of which can have serious environmental impact. This is where the use of an environmental management system can show the extent to which environmental issues are being considered in the manufacturing process.

- **Use:** how efficient is the product, what is the energy use pattern, the water use pattern and any suspected health and safety aspects? For example, fridges, freezers and washing machines now have scales to indicate the level of energy efficiency and water consumption·

- **Durability:** what is the life span of the product, how repairable is it, how likely is it to continue to be produced? Photocopiers and printers, for example, can have very different levels of performance and expectations of working life; one may be advertised as suiting, for example, offices with a requirement of 30,000 copies per month, whereas another model would handle 70,000 copies per month

- **Disposal:** how should the product be disposed of; how easy is it to be recycled; can it be collected separately from other waste, how damaging to the environment is its disposal? For example, batteries can at present simply be thrown away with the general waste; new legislation in the next few years, however, will control this because many types of battery contain acids and other hazardous chemicals.

The principles of environmental sound purchasing have been designed to be considered *before* you start any of the recognised purchasing stages (i.e. before the tender advertisement is placed). As a domestic purchaser, you would not just go out and make a purchase without first knowing what you were buying. The same can be said of environmental issues: you would not want to buy a product or service without first making all practicable efforts to research what buying that particular item means to the environment.

By applying the principles identified later in this section to the list of purchases that you are responsible for, you should find that there are two conclusions that can assist you in undertaking more environmentally aware purchasing. These are identified as:

■ The research carried out should help you identify the **current best practice** with regard to the environment and a particular purchase

■ From the resulting information you should be in a position to be able to **assign a level of environmental and profile risk** to a purchase.

By applying the principles of environmentally sound purchasing, any resultant information is typical only of the *current* best practice within industry. The scientific knowledge surrounding environmental issues, impacts associated with certain chemicals and the reactions involved, are continuously evolving. What may be regarded as good environmental practice today may be deemed less favourable tomorrow, when compared with a newer process. If a contract comes up for renewal or you are looking for new suppliers, it should not be assumed that because you have already researched the subject matter once that you do not need to do it again.

Following the supplier questionnaire are some general principles which should be applied. The questions posed are typical of what you should be looking for when making your purchase and should be treated as the minimum research needed rather than the final say.

8.3.2 Principles of environmentally sound purchasing

Sample questionnaire

1. Reduction
Reduction of the amount of material purchased: purchase only the amount that is required.
Can what you are looking to purchase be supplied in amounts that you require rather than in set amounts?   Yes ☐   No ☐   n/a ☐

2. Reusability
Emphasise the purchase of equipment which can be reused.
Can the purchase be reused?   Yes ☐   No ☐   n/a ☐

3. Re-engineerability
Select, wherever practicable, re-engineered equipment.
Is the equipment you're looking to purchase re-engineered?
        Yes ☐   No ☐   n/a ☐

4. Recyclability
Can the purchase be recycled?   Yes ☐   No ☐   n/a ☐
Is it easy to collect for recycling?   Yes ☐   No ☐   n/a ☐
Is the purchase designed to be recycled?   Yes ☐   No ☐   n/a ☐
Is the purchase itself recycled?   Yes ☐   No ☐   n/a ☐

5. Sourcing
Research where the materials have been sourced from and investigate whether this is the best, or only, option, with regards to the environment.
Have they come from a renewable (e.g. a forest) rather than a non-renewable resource (e.g. fossil fuel)?   Yes ☐   No ☐   n/a ☐
Is that source certified as being managed sustainably?
        Yes ☐   No ☐   n/a ☐
Can the purchase be viably sourced from a local supplier rather than be transported over large distances?   Yes ☐   No ☐   n/a ☐

6. Type
Look at the composition of what you are looking to purchase; determine whether you could actually be purchasing a less environmentally harmful alternative in terms of the materials used.
Have you researched into viable alternatives that might have a less environmentally harmful effect (e.g. NiH_2 batteries instead of NiCd)?
        Yes ☐   No ☐   n/a ☐
Is the purchase free of toxic or hazardous materials?
        Yes ☐   No ☐   n/a ☐

7 Manufacture
Determine how product (or products that a service uses) is manufactured.
Is the product (or product used as part of a service) consuming less energy in its production than alternatives (if any)?
        Yes ☐   No ☐   n/a ☐
Is the product consuming less water in its production than alternatives (if any)?   Yes ☐   No ☐   n/a ☐

8

Is the product emitting fewer pollutants into the surrounding air/water/land during its production than alternatives (if any)?

Yes ☐   No ☐   n/a ☐

8. Use
Determine how the product's usage during its life span affects the environment.
Is the purchase more efficient during its use, in terms of energy, water and any other resources consumed, than alternatives (if any)?

Yes ☐   No ☐   n/a ☐

Are all health and safety issues regarding the purchase known?

Yes ☐   No ☐   n/a ☐

9. Durability
It is better to purchase products/materials that are robust and less likely to become obsolete in a short period of time.
Is the purchase durable?   Yes ☐   No ☐   n/a ☐
If necessary can the purchase be repaired?   Yes ☐   No ☐   n/a ☐
Is it easy to repair?   Yes ☐   No ☐   n/a ☐

10. Disposal
How the product or wastes produced during the fulfilment of a service are disposed of.
Can the product or wastes be segregated before disposal?

Yes ☐   No ☐   n/a ☐

Can the product or any wastes be recycled?   Yes ☐   No ☐   n/a ☐
Are there recognised less environmentally harmful ways of disposing of the product or any wastes?   Yes ☐   No ☐   n/a ☐
Are these alternative disposal routes cost-efficient?

Yes ☐   No ☐   n/a ☐

These principles, and how you have answered the questions above, will be used when determining the degree of environmental risk associated with your purchase.

8.3.3 Supplier assessment questionnaire

This questionnaire is designed to enable your business gain a better understanding of your suppliers and the relative importance that the environment has within their activities. To do this it is split into three sections:

1. **Environmental management issues**

2. **Operations approach**

3. **Product/service delivered.**

All questions should be answered if possible – but of course some may not apply to your operation.

8

Supplier assessment questionnaire

Section 1: Environmental management issues

1a Does your company have an Environmental Management System such as ISO 14001 or EMAS?
Yes ☐ No ☐ Don't know ☐

If 'don't know', please find out.

1b Does your company have an environmental policy or statement of principles, which details your approach to environmental issues?
Yes ☐ No ☐ Don't know ☐

If yes, please submit a copy of such policies.

1c Does your company have a person responsible for environmental issues?
Yes ☐ No ☐ Don't know ☐

If yes, please provide the name of relevant employees:

1d Has your company undergone an environmental audit?
Yes ☐ No ☐ Don't know ☐

If yes, please provide the date(s):

1e Have employees at all levels undergone training to aid understanding of environmental issues, impacts and policies within the company?
Yes ☐ No ☐ Don't know ☐

If yes, please provide the date(s):

1f Has your company been prosecuted in relation to any environmental legislation in the last three years?
Yes ☐ No ☐ Don't know ☐

If yes, please provide details:

Section 2: Operations approach

2a Does your company monitor and regulate the following areas within its
operations?

Energy usage	Yes ❑	No ❑	Don't know ❑
Water usage	Yes ❑	No ❑	Don't know ❑
Solid waste	Yes ❑	No ❑	Don't know ❑

If **yes** to any of the above, please submit documentary evidence, such as
two or three years' worth of meter readings or records.

If **no** to any of the above, would you like information and assistance on how
to monitor and regulate?   Yes ❑   No ❑

2b Can your company readily identify the following as a percentage of your
annual turnover?

Energy consumption   _____   Water consumption   _____
Waste disposed of   _____   Raw materials   _____

If not, within what timescale can you make this data available?

2c Do you know what percentage of the raw materials used within your
operations are virgin (i.e. not used before)?
Yes ❑ % = _____   No ❑

2d Does your company use any recyclable or reusable materials, and if not are
there any processes in place to implement this?
                Yes ❑   No ❑   Don't know ❑

Section 3: Product/service delivered

3a Does the product or service that you provide contain or utilise any toxic or
hazardous materials?   Yes ❑   No ❑   Don't know ❑

If **yes**, is there any risk of rogue emissions to air, land, or water during use
and/or disposal?   Yes ❑   No ❑   Don't know ❑

Please submit documentation on any toxic or hazardous materials.

3b Has your company investigated the use of alternative materials, which are
less environmentally harmful, in the provision of your product or service?
                Yes ❑   No ❑   Don't know ❑
If **yes**, have you implemented these materials?   Yes ❑   No ❑

3c Is your company aware of any legislation (environmental) that covers the
manufacture or provision of your product or service?
                Yes ❑   No ❑
If **yes**, please submit a list of relevant legislation.

3d How does your company dispose of the waste generated during the
manufacture or provision of your product or service? (Please give details of
the different types of waste and how they are disposed.)

8.3.4 Issues to consider

Purchasing and supply is a very important function within an organisation. It defines for customers how they perceive the organisation and, if used properly by a purchaser, it can have a very powerful impact on the supplier. An effective environmental purchasing strategy cannot be fully implemented at a stroke; organisations should start slowly, and gradually address all purchases, rather than try to tackle everything at once.

Three key steps might be:

■ Address major purchases

■ Address purchases which have a major environmental impact

■ Address purchases which have a range of options, some of which have clear environmental alternatives.

Within the above topics, some detailed questions to consider and discuss with senior colleagues could include:

■ Are we satisfied with the performance of our suppliers?

■ Do we have too many suppliers?

■ Are there good communication channels between our company and suppliers?

■ Is environmental and quality management an issue for our company?

■ Is our company affected by environmental legislation? When did we last check?

■ Are we facing any risk of prosecution?

■ Is our company updated about current and imminent environmental trends?

■ Are we satisfied with our company's corporate performance? Can it be improved?

■ Are our customers satisfied with our company's performance? How do we know?

8.4 Sources of information

Chartered Institute of Purchasing and Supply
Sound approach to purchasing and supply.
www.cips.org

Environmental transport
Lots of information on greener motoring.
www.eta.co.uk

Ethical shopping   General advice.
www.responsibleshopper.org

Good Shopping Guide   Advice on informed decisions.
www.thegoodshoppingguide.co.uk

Supply Chain Environmental Management Programme
Practical benefits for companies. For more
information, look at the **Sustainable Supply
Chain Forum**:
http://sscf.info/DesktopDefault.aspx?tabid=52

and the **National Centre for Business and
Sustainability**:
www.thencbs.co.uk/
body_environmental_projects_10.html

Transport 2000   Campaigning organisation but useful
information.
www.transport2000.co.uk

Design and management of buildings and spaces

Case study

Having a building assessed to identify how good its environmental characteristics are, or where there is room for improvement, is one of the features of the Building Research Establishment's 'Environmental Assessment Method' (BREEAM). The assessment recognises best practice in design, construction and building management and should be seriously considered: not only for a new building, but also for an extension or even a refurbishment. (See www.bre.co.uk)

9

9.1 Overview

The contribution which buildings, the site and their management can make towards environmental good practice is often overlooked. In most city and urban industrial areas, we have become accustomed to buildings which are functional rather than attractive. There are too many sites which have some muddy grass and a few gaunt trees struggling to survive, which offer no value to the environment; many other sites are on parcels of land, from which old buildings have been removed, leaving the land contaminated and in need of remediation.

We spend most of our lives within one building or another; we rely on the building to provide us with an environment which is pleasant, safe and secure. Before the advent of effective heating , sewerage and ventilation schemes and electric light, most buildings had to work with the natural environment to maximise the benefits of sunlight, warmth and drainage. Although many of the older technologies were primitive – and many of the buildings were poorly constructed– they did exhibit many advantages over current constructions.

Our present ability to use an increasingly diverse range of construction materials, and the availability of technologies such as central heating, air conditioning, ventilation systems and double or triple glazing, has led us to construct buildings which rely on these technologies and which pay little heed to working with the natural environment. Buildings are constructed with substantial amounts of glass on all sides, and this allows heat out in the winter and excess heat in during the summer. Levels of insulation are often below what they could be, and the construction materials are often sourced from raw materials – sometimes on the other side of the planet – rather than using recycled, or locally sourced, materials. The buildings themselves, and associated car parking, are often sited on greenfield land, with the consequent loss of habitat and landscape. The wildlife habitats are replaced with tarmac and a few non-native trees and bushes which are unattractive to, or unsuitable for, the indigenous wildlife.

Buildings have a real opportunity to demonstrate a commitment to the concept of sustainability, as they can contribute positively to the environmental, financial and social aspects of sustainability:

■ The design can minimise the use of energy, water and other natural resources

■ Construction materials can be recycled

■ They can create space which is a benefit to wildlife.

Well-designed, environmentally sound buildings also make financial sense: the use of renewable energy sources, combined heat and power boilers, minimal air conditioning and reduced maintenance costs will all contribute to lower running costs which, over time, will demonstrate cost benefits over constructions built more cheaply but with higher running costs. In addition, a well-designed building will be a place where employees are pleased to work, contributing to lower absentee figures. The social benefits of sustainable buildings also accrue as they do not have a negative impact on health, are accessible to all – young, elderly and disabled – and should be attractive on the eye.

As older industrial buildings fall into disuse, the land on which they stand is frequently contaminated and requires remediation in order to be fit for new developments. Current remediation techniques usually involve the removal of soils to a special waste landfill site; new techniques involving bio-remediation are being developed, but the contribution these may make is unclear. However, this does stress the importance of not polluting land in the first place, because the cost of repairing damage can be considerable.

9.2 Building and space design

We can consider issues relating to design under several different headings:

- **The land**
- **Overall design**
- **Energy**
- **Water**
- **Internal environment**
- **Pollution**
- **Landscaping**
- **Access**
- **Crime prevention.**

We shall consider each of these in turn, and then provide a simple checklist to help you ensure that each element has been actively considered – even if it is later rejected.

9.2.1 The land

The Government is encouraging increased use of *brownfield* sites (that is, those that have been built on already and where the buildings have been removed); use of *greenfield* sites (sites which have not been built on) may require substantial discussions to obtain permissions and approvals. Consideration must be given to the proximity of public transport, as well as access for the type of delivery vehicles which the operation is likely to use or receive.

A site which can only easily be reached by car will require additional space and services (and hence cost) for provision of parking, and also reduce the availability of the workforce. There is also increasing awareness about flooding; at time of going to press the Environment Agency had just released updated mapping of the UK to show areas thought to be at risk.

In some instances the land may have pre-existing ecological or landscape features of value; ideally, the development should aim to enhance these. Developing brownfield land presents a major opportunity to address significant ecological gains.

9.2.2 The overall design

An increasing number of design companies and architects understand the principles of sustainable building design and can put these ideas into practice. In some instances it may be best to augment the general design with the expertise of particular designers who specialise in particular areas such as energy, materials, water, spatial needs for workers and ergonomics. This is of particular importance when designing with consideration for disabled people, the subject of recent UK legislation (the **Disability Discrimination Act 2003)**, which requires that new and existing non-domestic buildings are designed to be accessible to, and usable by, people with mobility and sensory impairments. There are also, of course, issues of security to consider, which can often be handled by natural or ecological measures rather than metal fences. Once a site has been identified, there are possibly three fundamental considerations:

- A fundamental design consideration is whether the building will go *upwards* – visually more obtrusive – or *outwards* – using more land. Planning control will obviously play a large part in determining this decision but there are environmental advantages and disadvantages in respect of each approach which need to be considered. If the building is a completely new construction, the *potential* for later extensions and modifications needs to be borne in mind

- Another general design consideration is the *aspect* of the building – that is, which way it faces. In trying to maximise incoming natural light – and reduce heat loss in winter – the idea of smaller windows on the north side and larger ones on the south-facing side would seem obvious. However, the additional heat created from this arrangement in summer might be undesirable, but a good designer should be able to produce the right balance

- Finally, in the general design, do not overlook the potential *views* which staff may have. The opportunity for staff to look out on an attractive environment should be facilitated and it would be desirable to reduce visibility of an unattractive view.

9.2.3 Energy

The cost of energy consumption is usually a building's major running cost; this cost is increasing and will continue to increase. Detailed consideration of energy issues is provided in Chapter 5. However, when constructing a new building, whether separate, an extension, or indeed a refurbishment, it is most cost-effective to install the best energy technology from the start. The capital cost of most energy systems with a high environmental performance is usually greater than the equivalent 'conventional' energy technology, but the running costs are always much lower; reasonably straightforward calculations can determine the payback period.

In performing these calculations, several points need to be borne in mind:

- The cost of energy in the UK in the next few years is set to rise significantly more than inflation

- The international political scene may further threaten security of supply with consequent further price rises

- A range of grants are available for installing energy-efficient systems

- Use of a combined heat and power system, able to use waste materials as a fuel source, should be considered, depending on the type of operations carried out.

Design of energy-efficient buildings – whether the energy is primarily used for heating, cooling or lighting – is now readily available and specialist contractors and architects can provide sound advice.

9.2.4 Water

Water costs are also significant for many businesses, especially those which use water as part of their production process. Even for offices, where water consumption is limited, the potential to make significant savings by installing efficient water-saving technology is worth doing.

As with energy minimisation, the opportunity to install modern and effective water technologies should be taken at the construction stage; the use of 'grey' water (from wash basins, washing machines or showers) for flushing toilets is now well established, as is the saving of rainwater. Rainwater can also be used for landscaped areas (and indeed is far better than mains water), as well as many manufacturing uses where water quality is not critical.

For businesses looking to retro-fit water-saving devices, a range of simple equipment is available from spray taps, to automatic turn-off taps, semi-flush and full-flush toilet systems and even waterless urinals.

9.2.5 Internal environment

Buildings aren't – or shouldn't be – just constructions built in splendid isolation. They are intended to be lived in and worked in; humans have needs, among which the most important are their physical comfort, well-being and psychological health. The term 'sick building syndrome' was coined in the 70s and 80s, after evidence accumulated that some buildings were so poorly designed that the people who lived or worked in them became physically, or even mentally, ill.

Consideration of the internal environment of a building should take into account the different level and type of lighting used, thermal comfort levels and the flexibility of usage which might be needed in the workspaces. Attention also needs to be given to the type (and, indeed, colour) of paint used on the walls, since certain types of paints give off fumes; the type of chemical cleaners used; carpeting or floor-coverings; and the many other issues which affect different people in different ways, such as the way air conditioning is employed and the availability of windows that can open. One of the drawbacks of the open-plan office is that it is invariably (and unsurprisingly!) designed as open plan, with lighting and air-flow patterns determined on that basis. In practice, however, many staff in open plan offices erect screens or filing cabinets as 'barriers' which then interfere with the lighting and air flow. There is clearly a balance to be struck between an open office (which aids communication, team working and is cheaper to build and clean) and coping with the needs of individuals who work in that office.

Recent studies have also demonstrated the extent to which indoor plants can contribute to a healthy atmosphere in the workplace. They emit oxygen during the daylight hours; their colour and smell can also help staff feel psychologically better.

9.2.6 Pollution

Attention needs to be paid to the extent to which pollutants created by the work in the building may affect the local area. These pollutants do not just include air and water pollutants but also include litter, dust and other physical materials as well as noise. It should also be borne in mind that, just because there may be no residential areas close by, issues of noise and other pollutants are not a concern. Other businesses may have a requirement for clean air or water, not only for the well-being of their staff but also for their manufacturing or operational processes.

9.2.7 Landscaping

If not already present, the area around a construction may have the potential to provide an attractive landscape or a useful area for wildlife. Very often in building developments, the construction company wishes to remove as much as possible to make life as easy as possible for building work; it may well remove useful and attractive bushes, trees, plants and herbs and wildlife areas. These natural features can be attractive, as well as providing helpful shading to the building; in some locations they may effectively screen the building from external view. Construction of a pond or wetland area would be very easy at the same time as the building goes up; such areas provide an excellent habitat for much wildlife and will provide interest for staff. Security considerations (see below, under crime prevention) encourage certain types of hedging.

Try to avoid opting for simple mown grass, with a few bushes and 'lollipop' trees; these will have limited landscape interest, low wildlife value and be relatively expensive to maintain. A well-designed natural area will not only be beneficial to all but will also be cost-effective to maintain. Although there may be an initial capital cost to create a landscaped area with different contours and different features, the maintenance costs are likely to be a lot lower than those of a conventional flat area.

For some really good examples of how ecology and landscape can be integrated with buildings Dutch towns offer good demonstrations and in particular a visit to Arnhem in the Netherlands is recommended. Many Dutch towns demonstrate how small wooded areas around blocks of flats and industrial estates can screen off such sites and provide a more pleasant perspective for the users. They also have some excellent examples of how small lakes can make built-up areas more attractive. In several continental countries, 'habitat bridges' are being constructed over new motorways, in order to act as a wildlife corridor from one side to the other.

9.2.8 Access

As previously indicated, the location of the site in relation to public transport and good cycle routes is important. Predicted increases in car ownership and use and the resultant effect on road conditions could cause serious problems for businesses.

It is also important to consider access and facilities for disabled people, as well as the elderly and less able. New buildings must cater for disabled people and techniques and approaches are continually improving.

9.2.9 Crime prevention

Another area in which expertise has been developing rapidly over the past few years is the use of building design as an aid to crime prevention. Police crime prevention officers can provide advice on this, but issues such as designing the car park so that it can easily be seen from the buildings, avoidance of 'hidden corners', effective (but not polluting) lighting and security systems for the building such as pass codes on doors are also relevant.

Security is also an area where landscaping can play a significant part. Planting of a wide range of 'prickly' bushes as a 'first line of defence' is now well practised: where these are planted below windows, they prevent people getting too close and inhibit any passage into or out of the building. Many offices experience frequent thefts of handbags and equipment left adjacent to open windows, and these opportunistic crimes would be prevented by such defensive hedging. Water features around buildings may be a very effective modern form of moat, and prevent vehicles approaching from unauthorised directions; high banks can screen the building from casual view and deter opportunistic thefts of and from vehicles, as well as preventing much noise pollution .

9.3 Considerations for your business

9.3.1 The overall design

Good design of buildings is important for their effective operation and the health and welfare of the staff. In the last few years, there have been many developments and changes which radically affected the design of buildings, their materials, energy sources, landscaping, access and crime prevention. The overall aim of the whole process, whether the design and construction of a new building, the refurbishment of an old building or part of a building, is now to achieve an environmentally responsible design.

There are opportunities, whenever a company moves to new premises or furbishes a building, to consider incorporating environmentally sensitive design and construction techniques. Key design issues should focus on energy requirements which minimise energy consumption and maximise the individual user's environmental control. It should be possible at this stage to identify, at least approximately, the costs of these decisions – both capital and running costs. It is always useful to carry out a cost/benefit analysis, comparing different options. For buildings, the time frame for a cost/benefit analysis should be over an acceptably long period.

Solutions to environmental problems in facilities are as multidimensional as the problems; no single approach is likely to be fully effective, and no individual can resolve the problem alone. The approach should involve architects, management, facility managers, designers, engineers, caretakers and your own staff, who should all have reasonable environmental awareness and knowledge and understand their role in the project.

Here is a simple checklist of questions, which should be considered at the earliest stage. There is no 'correct' answer; rather they are ideals to which one should work, everything else being equal. What is, perhaps, crucial is that the issues have been fully considered at a time when they *could* be implemented or adopted – rather than when it is too late or too expensive to adopt them. You should be able to defend any construction or refurbishment issue on the basis that all of the options were considered, and those which had a cost/benefit were adopted – and that other options were only rejected after due reflection.

9.3.2 Design and facility requirements

■ Does the facility need to be built – or are there facilities that can be adapted for reuse?

■ How can heat and energy be reduced, recovered and recycled?

■ Can site selection criteria be identified which minimise environmental disturbances, such as modifying the existing site features or scenic vistas, or which threaten rare or delicate ecosystems?

■ Can environmental characteristics for building materials be specified?

■ Can composting and recycling opportunities be identified and, if so, can the potential volumes and types of materials generated by the project be estimated? Can space to accommodate their storage be planned in?

■ Can the major energy requirements of the building be satisfied using renewable energy sources?

9.3.3 Site selection

■ What habitat or other ecological damage will occur if the site is built upon?

■ Has there been adequate site testing, including for hazardous materials, to determine if the site can be safely developed?

■ How will the site cope with rainfall or possible flooding? Will soakaways be used or standard drainage?

■ What wastes could be treated onsite?

■ Is the site sufficiently large to incorporate habitat and environmental conservation of existing features or the development of new habitats?

9.3.4 Building design and orientation

■ Have environmental solutions been costed and their payback period and cost/benefits realistically established?

- Have publications from the Building Research Establishment (BRE) been studied?

- How flexible is the facility with regard to alternative uses and future developments?

- Has the orientation of the building been adjusted to maximise natural environmental benefits and minimise losses?

9.3.5 Building material and product selection

- Has life cycle assessment of major materials been undertaken or information about them sought and acted upon?

- Are all the features of the building essential? Where not essential, have additional environmental criteria been applied?

- Is the building likely to contain any materials from endangered, exotic, non-renewable or otherwise unsustainable sources?

- Will (or does) the building contain hazardous materials, or use hazardous materials in construction that may prove difficult to dispose of?

- Has the building been designed to be low maintenance?

- Have you required the builder to purchase exactly to specification and minimise over-ordering?

- Have you examined the use of recycled materials wherever possible?

- Are materials being sourced locally?

- Is the wood used from sustainably managed forests? Can this be verified and certified?

- Is the preservation treatment of the wood carried out using environmentally sound methods and chemicals?

- Have you considered carpet materials which can be retextured (i.e. to have any stain- and water-resistant treatments added back during cleaning)?

- What will happen to the carpet offcuts?

- Are paints water-based rather than solvent-based?

9.3.6 Energy

- Is the equipment and system designed to be energy efficient?

- Is the equipment designed for easy maintenance and repair?

- Is the required maintenance environmentally harmful?

- Have sustainable energy supplies been incorporated, such as solar panels and photovoltaics?
- Has a combined 'heat and power' boiler been specified?
- Have all the available grants for energy supply been investigated?
- Have greenhouse gases been excluded from the air conditioning system?
- Are automatic switches and controls installed wherever possible?
- Has a voltage reduction stabiliser been assessed?
- Has the *detail* of lighting requirements been considered, looking at the design, layout, configuration, controllability and types of lighting?

  As a guide to the levels of energy consumption to be achieved, a cost of around £4 per square metre is a good target. However, in an air-conditioned office, good practice would allow for a cost of around £8 per square metre. (Source, EnergyTrust – see 9.5, Sources of information)

9.3.7 Ventilation

- Has the ventilation for the building been optimised?
- Can the ventilation be easily adjusted manually? Does it allow individuals to adjust it for their work area?
- What are the likely indoor air quality issues?
- How will you assess the indoor air quality – and if unsatisfactory will you be able to do anything about it?
- Have you specified that volatile organic compounds (VOCs) must not be used in the construction or fitting process?
- Are locations available for siting of indoor plants ?
- How will siting of cabinets and screens, especially within open plan areas, affect the overall air movement and ambience of the spaces in the building?

9.3.8 Landscaping

- Has the site landscape been considered alongside the building design?
- Have existing features, notably trees, been specifically preserved?
- Has the car parking area been well screened with pollution-tolerant species?
- Have native plants been preferred and/or have beneficial insect-attracting species been selected?

- Have drought-tolerant species been identified?

- If an atrium is included in the design, have suitable species been identified and can a 'grey water' system be used for watering?

- Will the landscaping and habitats link with other habitats nearby to make 'wildlife corridors'?

9.3.9 Specifications and documentation

- Have you specified that the environmental performance of suppliers, constructors and materials be assessed using *pro formas* as in Chapter 8?

- Where claims are made, have these been verified?

- Has an architect and designer been selected who has experience, awareness and knowledge about environmentally sustainable buildings?

- Will the manufacturers of building products take back unused materials?

- Does the manufacturer offer a range of products, with differing environmental properties?

- Can the packaging of products be reduced, reused or eliminated altogether?

9.3.10 Waste management

- If an existing building is being wholly or partially demolished, what is happening to the materials? Are they being reused (at this site or another)?

- If a brownfield site is being used, how is the soil being remediated – and what is happening to the waste material?

- Have manufacturers and builders discussed with you how they will manage their waste?

- Have contacts been made with a building materials bank?

- Have all staff been trained in waste control issues?

- How will hazardous waste will be handled, disposed of or recycled?

9.3.11 Facility management

- Has the building been designed to minimise cleaning?

- Has a cleaning company been selected which uses materials with limited environmental impact?

- Are containers of cleaning materials reusable; are cleaning materials purchased in bulk?

- Are all cleaning chemicals and materials stored in a properly locked and marked cupboard?

- Are dust-reduction techniques used in the cleaning?

- Are air vents and ducts cleaned on a regular basis?

- Are cleaners expected to maintain plants?

- Do cleaners report maintenance problems, such as dripping taps?

- Are cleaning staff instructed about switching off lighting and heating?

9.4 Summary

The management of buildings is dependent upon the design and building specifications, but, regrettably, buildings which have been constructed with consideration for the site and the efficiency of use and management are still very few. The provision of buildings where the amount of glass is the same on the north as the south side results in excessive use of heat in winter and excessive use of air conditioning in summer. Alternatives include the replacement of some of the glass by walls, properly insulated – and, even better, by photovoltaic systems to allow the generation of electricity from a sustainable source. The problem is that to design and construct a building to higher environmental standards is more expensive in terms of initial capital – though it results in significantly reduced running and maintenance costs. Where the design and construction company is different from the company using the building, there is little pressure to improve construction quality.

Building management is an area where most organisations can make significant contribution to reducing any negative environmental impact. The use of energy in many modern buildings is enormous – yet lack of efficient controls and lack of staff awareness is frequently a problem, and an impediment to making immediate improvements. There are many buildings around in which the heating controls are located on the middle floor, the result being that those on the lower floors tend to be too cold and those on the upper floors tend to be too warm. In many buildings, the most important people in control of energy use are caretakers and cleaners: these individuals switch on the lights in the morning and frequently nobody switches them off until the caretaker goes round at night to secure the building. Building management also includes the cleaning of the offices and toilets and the provision of places for collecting and storing materials for recycling. Recent research looking at the role of vegetation within buildings has demonstrated the considerable benefits (aesthetic, atmospheric and health) which occur when plants are grown within offices.

Outside the building itself, the site offers significant potential for contributing to environmental improvement. The use of trees and hedges within car parks and in the front area are frequently overlooked; when some of this landscaping *is* tackled, it is frequently with plants which are unattractive to insects or birds. A more concerted approach is needed to develop our urban landscape in a way which is not only attractive but also has ecological values.

This chapter has tried to cover a wide range of the environmental issues involved in building design, construction and use. It is highly unlikely that your business will be in a position to use *all* of the BPEO techniques, but even addressing a single issue is advantageous.

Given the choice, careful management of energy and reduction in its use is likely to result in the biggest financial payback.

9.5 Sources of information

Association for Environment Conscious Building

Low-cost membership for useful information.
www.aecb.net

Building Research Establishment

Leading independent organisation in UK
providing expert advice on building
construction and management.
www.bre.co.uk

Centre for Sustainable Design

The Centre acts as an information clearing
house and a focus for innovative thinking on
sustainable products and services.
www.cfsd.org.uk

Construction Industry Research and Information Association

Includes information on brownfield land.
www.ciria.org.uk

Contaminated land   Information on contaminated land.
www.contaminatedland.co.uk

Institution of Civil Engineers

Look in particular at the section on
'sustainability' which it defines as 'meeting
the needs of today without compromising
those of tomorrow'.
www.ice.org.uk

The Wildlife Trusts   Information on caring for wildlife habitats
www.wildlifetrusts.org

Developing an environmental policy

Case study

Brightwater Engineering, a supplier of filtration systems to the water industry, recognised that it was actually operating in the field of environmental improvement – and that having an environmental policy would enable it to improve upon its already-positive impact upon the environment, help it to keep existing contracts and acquire new ones.

One of the main filtration materials developed by Brightwater was manufactured from recycled plastic; the development of an environmental policy allowed the company to realise the benefits of highlighting that particular feature among its other environmental aims.

10

10.1 Overview

An environmental policy sets out the commitment to the environment and the aims and aspirations of the organisation in terms of improving its relationship to the environment. Increasingly, businesses are being asked to show their environmental policy and to demonstrate how they are putting it into practice. This is particularly so for major organisations which have established an Environmental Management System (EMS) (see Chapter 11 for more information on this) and which are therefore imposing environmental standards on their suppliers.

A good environmental policy will have a relationship with several other policies, notably health and safety, training policy and quality. As with these other policies, the environmental policy should be written for your organisation: it has to mean what it says and say what it means. The policy should also set out what your organisation is trying to achieve and what your organisation's beliefs are in respect of the environment.

An environmental policy is often compared to a health and safety policy or quality management policy: the three are similar, in that they all aim at identifying, monitoring and improving aspects of a company's performance. However the environmental policy is different from the other two in its underlying aims: health and safety and quality policies lead to strategies with clearly defined *quantitative* objectives, such as zero accidents or zero defects. An environmental policy tends to lead to *qualitative* objectives – though many of these may be monitored quantitatively: an improvement, within the policy, may be concerned with reducing energy consumption but, in order to measure this reduction, annual readings need to be taken and specific (quantitative) targets set. There is no requirement which stipulates exactly what an environmental policy should achieve other than the resulting environmental strategy should contribute to the overall improvement of the organisation in terms of reducing its environmental impacts.

In some circumstances you may feel that it is realistic to identify weaknesses in your organisation; companies which specialise in topics which are environmentally sensitive, such as energy or chemicals, may therefore set out a policy statement which recognises that they:

> '... will continue to monitor and investigate the Best Practicable Environmental Option relating to ...*(their particular field)'*.

There are several pressures on businesses which are requiring them to set out environmental policies for their organisation:

■ Insurance companies are, increasingly, asking to see environmental policies in addition to their previous requests to see health and safety policies and other policies

- Many customers and clients are now asking suppliers about their environmental policies; this is particularly true of utility companies, local authorities, and large companies, all of which have significant opportunity to have a negative (or, hopefully, a positive) impact on the environment

- Companies which want to export, particularly to Europe, are expected to have environmental policies.

10.2 Environmental policies: the rationale

10.2.1 The need for an environmental policy

The purpose of an environmental policy for your organisation is that it should be able to demonstrate (to those who work within your organisation and those outside your organisation) what you believe in as a company, and what you are trying to achieve. It should also:

- Show that your organisation meets legislative requirements

- Consider the demands of other stakeholders

- Improve profitability

- Enhance the environment – locally, regionally and globally

- Be feasible and practical to implement

- Be checked regularly and changed as needed

- Keep up with changing commercial, legislative and societal demands.

10.2.2 Who needs an environmental policy?

The environment affects all organisations, regardless of size or sector, and therefore an environmental policy is a very useful statement as to how your organisation responds to the environment.

If your company is part of a larger organisation, it may be that there is a policy appropriate for the whole group. However, even if you are part of a larger group it is highly likely that your company has significant differences from the centre or from other branches, and therefore it would be more realistic to draw up an environmental policy, based on the group policy, but referring to the particular issues relevant to your site.

10.2.3 What does an environmental policy contain?

There tends to be an accepted pattern to most environmental policies.

- They are printed on headed paper

- They usually contain an initial paragraph which describes the nature and general principles of the company

■ There are a series of statements which set out the practices, or aims or particular principles, relating to individual areas of the company's operations. For most companies there will be statements relating to the following topics:

- compliance with all relevant legislation

- reduction of waste, and/or increase in recycling

- reduction of energy consumption

- transport improvement strategies

- training of staff

- research into new and improved techniques and equipment relevant to their business

- reduction of pollution

- the link with health and safety performance

- consumption of resources relevant to their business

- selection of the type of resources relevant to their business.

There may, of course, be other topics that you consider relevant.

An example of an environmental policy for a small company is shown on the following pages.

10

Fisher Research Ltd
ENVIRONMENTAL POLICY STATEMENT

Environmental Management System

Document No.:   Page: Revision No.:   Date issued:

Compiled by: Signed:

Authorised by: Signed:

Environmental Policy

Fisher Research Limited recognises that the pursuit of economic growth and a healthy environment must be closely linked.

Fisher Research Limited's Environmental Policy aims at integrating sound environmental practices into its operation. The policy has the following principles:

- *Regulations and Legislation:*

  To be fully aware of the requirements of all relevant current regulations and legislation and work with the appropriate authorities and organisations to achieve this, and to be aware of new and future legislation.

- *Waste:*

  To seek to minimise waste and promote waste recycling and the use of recycled materials, especially for packaging associated with the products it manufactures or supplies.

- *Energy and Resources:*

  To monitor the energy used in its operations and areas and install energy-saving practices.

  To take positive action on raw material and water consumption in order to preserve, as far as is practicable, natural resources.

- *Discharges and Emissions:*

  To reduce or eliminate as far as it is possible discharges and emissions to air, land and water, by improving processes, treatments and minimising risk.

- *Pollution Risk:*

  To take all the necessary actions to reduce pollution risk by:

  - improving all the areas where hazardous products are used or stored

- following strict procedures for storage and handling of hazardous products

- controlling and checking on a regular basis all processes and materials using or containing hazardous products

- devising emergency plans or procedures to deal with potential accidents or hazards.

- *Products:*

To continually review the environmental impacts of the products it manufactures or supplies and to work to reduce harmful impacts by research or developing new products.

- *Suppliers and Customers:*

To work as far as possible with suppliers and contractors to identify the best environmental practices and to high environmental standards.

To strive to give customers the best available information to enable them to use their products in a healthy environmental condition.

- *Organisation:*

To integrate in the company's organisation an environmental structure, to ensure this policy will carry out, and follow through, environmental performance improvements.

To provide appropriate environmental training for all the company's staff.

To ensure that all employees are aware that poor practices can result in hazards and risk to both the health and safety of employees and to the environment.

To review and update this policy on a regular basis to ensure environmental issues arising from new developments are integrated in this policy.

To conduct on a regular basis the audit and review of the company's environmental performance to assess progress and identify any deficiency in order to correct it.

- *Communication:*

To communicate this policy to the staff, the suppliers, the customers and other persons that could be interested (e.g. insurance company, bank).

- *Other aspects that Fisher Research Limited will instigate:*

To seek to start an Environmental Management System.

To prepare an annual report of the company's environmental and health and safety performance.

Reproduced by kind permission of Fisher Research Ltd

10.2.4 Presenting your environmental policy

As with many aspects of life, the way something is presented can be as impressive as the content. Some companies produce their environmental policy within a small booklet; others more simply, on a sheet of headed paper; and others reproduce it on their website.

You could see some examples of how other companies produce their environmental policies by visiting their websites and downloading or requesting copies of their printed material. By way of example, here are three very different major companies – with very different environmental impacts:

- Unilever (www.unilever.com, then check out its 'environment and society' page, which has its environmental report as a downloadable document)

- British Airports Authority (www.baa.com, then click on 'sustainability')

- McDonald's (www.mcdonalds.co.uk, click on 'good works' and then 'our environment', and then download a copy of 'Our Environmental Policy'.

10.2.5 Writing an environmental policy

The first step in developing an environmental policy is to obtain a detailed understanding of how your organisation relates to the environment. The best way to do this is to carry out an environmental review of your organisation. This provides an opportunity to gain an overview of the organisation's impacts on the environment and provides a baseline for monitoring improvements in the future.

Later in this chapter is a pro forma which you may wish to complete to provide you with a thorough picture of the environmental issues of your organisation. There are many versions of such an environmental review but this is one we have developed at CESMB and used on many occasions; it seems to work well. We would suggest you consider carefully who you ask to carry out this review, as a completely objective view is needed. A newly appointed manager, a senior member of staff from one department examining another department, or an independent outsider would all be ideal candidates, if they have reasonable environmental knowledge.

This environmental review should then be turned into a report. A succinct way of doing this would be to write the report as an environmental analysis, identifying the strengths, weaknesses, opportunities and threats (SWOT) which the review has identified.

From this SWOT report an environmental policy can be drafted.

10.2.6 Who is involved in the environmental policy?

As with most other policies, the environmental policy requires understanding and response from all staff, but there are some key staff who need direct involvement in drafting and implementation of the environmental policy:

■ **Director** – there should be one member of the board of directors who signs off the final version of the policy and who is responsible for ensuring that the company addresses the different aspects of the policy

■ **Senior manager** – responsible for ensuring that the different parts of the policy are implemented

■ **Health and safety manager** – it is necessary for this manager to be aware of the relationship and implications between the H&S policy and the environmental policy

■ **Departmental heads** – important for them to understand how the environmental policy applies to their area of work

■ **Environment team staff** – many organisations put selected members of staff into an environmental team or working party which might act variously as a ginger group, ideas group or advisory group.

10.2.7 What else does an environmental policy need?

An environmental policy should be more than just a document; if you do not treat it as a signpost for pointing your business in the direction you want to go, then that is all it will remain.

To turn the environmental policy statements into action, several steps are needed:

■ **Staff involvement:** many of the statements in your environmental policy are likely to rely, at least in part, on action by staff. This might include simple actions such as switching off lights, driving differently or segregating waste ready for recycling. Investing in staff training and practising effective communication is important

■ **Investment:** it is likely that some investment may be needed in order to kick-start some of the policy aims, or to achieve some of the objectives in the policy. However, it would be wrong to see this as 'the environment costing money', as some traditional views have it; rather, it should be seen as investment for increasing efficiency and business improvement. Some of that investment may be in new equipment and improved technologies, whereas +other investment may be in staff time

■ **Identification of priorities and development of an action plan:** nobody expects your business to do everything you need or want to do all at once; you should develop a clear action plan and take a step-by-step improvement journey, which might last a year or more

■ **An annual report:** this sets out what has been achieved each year and what is proposed for the next year.

In addition to the above it is also useful to set out an environmental management document – this should be clearly set out on headed paper and provide details of how environmental issues are managed in the company. The sections that might be addressed are:

■ Organisational structure

■ Environmental responsibility: staff, positions, areas of responsibility

■ Improvement objectives: developed from the policy

■ Maintenance objectives: developed from the policy

■ Staff environmental training record

■ Annual targets: developed from the objectives

■ Record of annual achievements: looking back at targets, then setting the next year's targets.

10.3 Environmental policies: the first steps

The first step to producing an environmental policy is to get a good idea of what the environmental issues are that you face in your business, ideally by carrying out an **environmental review**.

10.3.1 Environmental review – pro forma

This is a format for carrying out an environmental review. In most instances it indicates why topics are important and suggests the issues to be examined. The purpose of the review is to identify the ways in which an organisation affects the environment and how the environmental factors affect the organisation.

The review is essentially a qualitative study: it describes rather than measures. It will identify key factors and, where possible, future trends. The report will also try to highlight areas where potential savings may be made.

Environmental review pro forma

Organisation details

A: Organisation information

Company name: Contact name:

Address: Tel:
                                 Company size:

B: Organisation's activity
Describe the company activity, including products/services, transport used, packaging used, recycling, re-engineering; also describe any prescribed processes. Indicate if the organisation is part of a larger group.

C: Management structure and organisation
For an effective implementation of environmental practices in an organisation, there needs to be someone with responsibility for environmental affairs; they should have clear levels of responsibility and be able to report to senior colleagues regarding decisions. It is also common practice to have a group of staff representing different departments in the organisation to contribute to environmental knowledge and developments.

- Is there an organisational chart for the company?

- Is there a member of senior staff with responsibility for environmental affairs in the organisation? If not, how are environmental affairs decided, documented and defined?

- If there is a member of staff with responsibility for environmental issues, who do they report to, and where are decisions made?

- Where are policies, documents and other information stored? How accessible are they for staff?

D: Policies
The policies published by an organisation are a reflection of its aims and aspirations and the extent to which it is trying to put identified strategies into place. Although a policy is a piece of paper, it will need to be demonstrated how it is being put into place, and how it is reported, reviewed and documented. The policies will also be a reflection of the main concerns and areas of operation of the organisation.

- What policies does the organisation already have: Environmental? Health and Safety? Quality? Note any others that are relevant.

- Are these policies published – and if so, where?

- How are staff, the public and your customers made aware of your policies?

- How are the policies implemented; who checks them?

10

Operational details

E: Product and process design
Adopting a cradle-to-grave approach to considering a product will include consideration of the design of the product. The process by which a product is manufactured is also important and should lead to consideration of how the process can be carried out in a more sustainable manner.

- Can the design of the product be changed?

- Are any products (or elements of products) subject to environmental legislation?

- Can the product be made with less energy or water or by using recycled materials?

- Can the packaging be redesigned and reduced?

- What is the potential for repair, re-engineering or recycling of the product?

- Are BPEO and BATNEEC principles applied to the product and its manufacturing process?

F: Materials, supplies and suppliers
The materials, resources and supplies that an organisation uses are an important aspect of the environmental impact. A tendency to identify and use recycled or re-engineered materials; to reuse materials; and to check on the environmental attitude and performance of suppliers is an indication of the environmental awareness of the organisation.

- What raw materials are used, and what is the source of these materials?

- What consideration is given to environmentally sound alternatives? How are these investigated and considered?

- How is material use controlled? How are potential savings from resource efficiency identified, and are reverse logistics considered?

- What controls can be exerted over suppliers? By whom and how (and when and how often) does this take place?

- Are any hazardous materials used? Can these be substituted, by more environmentally sound materials?

- What recycled or recovered materials could be used? Have these been investigated?

G: Storage
Legislation does exist for some materials but it is important that all materials should be properly stored, information about the materials documented, and a clear emergency procedure developed for use in the event of abnormal situations.

■ Is storage compliant with legislation?

■ List storage of hazardous materials, and any other items of concern, in the table below.

Material	Purpose	Controls	Location	Disposal

■ How often are stored materials checked? Are all materials properly labelled?

■ Are stored areas adequately bunded, and are bunds maintained?

■ Are storage areas reasonably secure?

■ What are the emergency procedures in the event of abnormal situations?

■ Any pressurised tanks?

H: Energy

Consumption of energy is a major cost for many organisations, and also a major opportunity for cost savings. The future trend is likely to be that energy costs will rise as an attempt to control carbon emissions.

■ What is energy used for?

■ What forms of energy are used?

■ What energy minimisation measures are used? What additional ones could be used?

■ How is energy use monitored?

■ What are the main areas of energy waste?

■ What is the potential for using combined heat/power boilers, solar power, landfill gas or other alternative forms of energy?

■ Are energy costs apportioned by section/department?

I: Water

Water can be used in large quantities. For most firms their water supply is metered so there is an incentive to control its use.

■ For what purposes is water used in the operation?

10

■ Where is water sourced?

■ What has been done to reduce water waste? What is the potential for this?

■ Is there potential to recycle or reuse water?

■ Are any materials discharged through the water?   Is there consent – and what about materials not consented? Fill in the table below.

Material discharged	From what process	Monitoring	Legislation

■ Is water discharge monitored – and are discharges to water monitored?

■ Are all pipes checked regularly for leaks?

■ Is any onsite treatment of water carried out?

■ What alternative power sources are available in the event of emergency?

■ What is the emergency plan if systems fail?

J: Emissions to atmosphere
The control of air quality is the responsibility of local authorities, using strict legislation set out by the Government. It is an area of law which is being progressively tightened.

■ Are any materials (including dusts) emitted to air?

Pollutant source	Emission point	Abatement devices	Monitoring

■ How are emission levels reported, and how regularly?

■ Note any previous incidents of uncontrolled releases.

■ Describe plans for new abatement technology in relation to forthcoming technology.

■ What are the emergency plans in the event of an abnormal situation?

K: Waste

All organisations produce waste. The costs of waste disposal are increasing and are likely to continue to do so. The aim of any organisation moving towards sustainability is to reduce its resource use and minimise the wastes being disposed of.

■ Where are waste materials stored? Is their storage compatible with good housekeeping, good site operation and does it minimise risk of accidents?

■ Complete the table below.

Waste type	Waste source	Waste quantity	Principal component	Treatment

■ Are waste streams monitored? When, by whom, how often and how reported?

■ Are waste contractors used? Who, how often, what alternatives have been investigated?

■ Where is waste transfer documentation?

■ What alternatives to disposal might there be? What is the potential for recycling, or returning materials or equipment?

■ Is the organisation affected by packaging regulations?

■ Complete a waste reduction opportunities chart.

L: Transport

A key environmental area, and one likely to pose questions to every organisation.

■ What transport is used?   Specify what for, and approximate costs involved.

■ How are vehicles maintained?

■ What is the company's vehicle policy? Is public transport, cycling and shared car use encouraged? How?

■ What controls are placed on drivers of delivery/company vehicles, such as parking, speed limits?

M: Noise

■ Is noise an issue? What protection is available for staff, visitors, general public?

■ Have there been complaints?

10

N: Facilities management
Buildings all need looking after and this can have significant environmental impact.

■ Comment on heating, lighting, cleaning, furnishings, decorating, fittings, etc.

■ Also comment on external features, car park, landscaping and site management.

O: Site management
The way an organisation manages its site is important, both in the control of discharges and emissions from the site, and also in the overall appearance and the way that visitors view the organisation.

■ What is the history of the site?

■ What (and where) are the drains on the site? Where do they go – and are there any interceptors? Is there a readily accessible plan of the underground pipes, drainage and tanks on the site?

■ What are the storage facilities on the site? How susceptible are they to wind blow of waste?

■ Is the site near to any ecologically interesting sites, either land or water? How does the site impact on these or other areas?

■ What are the flood and emergency rainfall discharge measures?

■ Is there any evidence or risk of land contamination?

Management issues

P: Training
Training in environmental understanding, awareness and knowledge is necessary in order to spread the environmental strategy throughout the organisation. Training should also be a two-way process, encouraging and equipping staff to contribute to the environmental improvement process.

■ What environmental training is provided and to whom?

■ What environmental training is provided to staff in key positions (i.e. those who might have to deal with an emergency or abnormal condition)?

■ What environmental information is provided to new staff?

■ Is environmental performance included in appraisals?

■ How environmentally aware and committed are staff? What are the indicators of this?

Q: Public relations
This includes how the company is seen by the public, how it tries to portray its green image, and what links it develops with local communities and how it affects neighbours.

- What environmental information does the company publish? Is this included with other materials or separate?

- What information is available to inquirers?

- How does the organisation deal with complaints? Are these logged?

- What contacts and relationships does the organisation have with local communities and neighbours? How far does this extend? What is the aim of these links and contacts?

R: Financial matters
This includes the investment, insurance and any purchasing policies that the organisation has. Current trends show significant interest in ethical investments.

- Are environmental issues considered when planning budgets and, if so, how? Who is making the decisions in this area?

- Is there consideration of environmental issues when investing in new equipment, sites or businesses? Is the purchase made only on the cheapest criteria or do environmental issues get considered?

- What environmental questions are raised when purchasing new equipment or materials?

- What is the organisation's insurance against environmental accidents?

- How are environmental savings identified in the finance controls – for example, is a cost/benefit analysis applied?

S: Marketing
- Are the products and services attractive to 'green' consumers?

- Are the sales staff aware of green consumer interest in products similar to yours?

- If the product or process were changed, would there be any market advantage?

10

10.3.2 The environmental review report

The environmental review report will contain the following sections:

- Description of what is happening in the organisation
- Highlighting of good practice
- Highlighting of areas for improvement
- Potential for waste minimisation (includes wastage of material, energy, water and possibly staff)
- Further contacts.

The waste minimisation section will look at:

- The waste material being produced
- Alternative options to the waste material
- Alternatives to the current waste disposal
- Estimates of the cost savings where possible
- Recommendations for any equipment investment to gain savings.

10.3.3 Turning the report into a policy

Use the environmental review to address the key issues for the environmental policy. You should remember that it is just as important to include *positives* in the policy as it is to include *negatives*. The policy should be a realistic reflection of what your organisation is doing and what it is aiming to achieve.

It is also well worthwhile looking at a few examples of environmental policies available on company websites, as detailed earlier in this chapter.

And finally don't forget to:

- Date the policy
- Get it signed by a director
- Review it on a regular (usually annual) basis.

10.4 Summary

The environment now constitutes an important commercial pressure, requiring changes in corporate activity and style. It is *people* that are the key to helping improve the environmental performance of organisations. By adopting a formal environmental policy with appropriate commitment, the environment can be given the importance that is needed to achieve sustainability.

10.5 Sources of information

ENDS Report   Environmental Data Services – a leading
                                 environment business journal: lots of
                                 information on what other companies are
                                 doing.
                                 www.endsreport.com

Environment Industry Yearbook
                                 A very useful publication listing all types of
                                 environmental product and service for
                                 businesses.
                                 www.eiy.co.uk

Environmental survey   Summary of larger document but with
                                 comments about company environmental
                                 policy in general.
                                 www.pirc.co.uk/pubs/env99

Envirowise   Free publications on writing environmental
                                 policy.
                                 www.envirowise.gov.uk

Howarth Timber   How one company addresses wood as a
                                 resource.
                                 www.howarth-timber.co.uk

Institution of Environmental Sciences
                                 www.ies-uk.org.uk

Norfolk   Basic advice about writing an environmental
                                 policy.
                                 www.norfolk.gov.uk/environment/
                                 nccenvpolicy.htm

10

Sample policies   Look at websites of any major company; some
                                 examples include **Pearson, Sony Music** and
                                 Canon. In first two cases, look under
                                 'environment' on the home page.
                                 www.pearson.com   www.sonymusic.co.uk

                                 For Canon, follow the links to 'About us',
                                 'Annual report' and then to 'environmental
                                 activities'.
                                 www.canon.co.uk

Environmental management systems

Case study

Royde and Tucker, a company based in north London, manufactures high-quality door fittings, such as hinges, pivots and letterplates. It recently took over a plating plant in Hitchin but needed to take urgent steps to improve parts of the operation – and the company also knew that in a year or two it would need to apply for an IPPC certificate. By developing an environmental management system simultaneously with its work on health and safety systems, the company was able to identify and focus on its most significant operations and to integrate them into the overall management of the site.

11

11.1 Overview

The development of management systems, which are designed to give managers control over the processes taking place within the organisation, are a feature of the last 25 years. Although different approaches to management have been proposed for many decades, it was not until the early 1980s, with the development of the Quality Management System (QMS), that these approaches came to be more widely adopted.

In the early 1990s an Environmental Management System (EMS) was developed which aimed to assist businesses (primarily manufacturing) to control the environmental performance of their operation. There are now several offshoots of the original system, which address topics such as environmental performance, auditing and other more specialist topics.

11.1.1 BS 7750 and ISO 14001

The EMS was originally developed in the UK by the British Standards Institute (BSI) as BS 7750, as a means of identifying and controlling the environmental impacts of an organisation. It is also intended to allow the organisation to set out its policies for the future. Simultaneously, the European Union established a similar system, now known as the Environmental Management and Audit Scheme (EMAS), though this required that a public statement of the environmental performance of the organisation is required. By the turn of the century, the International Standards Organisation (ISO) had adopted the UK system, now known as ISO 14001; moves were also afoot to combine this with the EU's EMAS system, to create a universal certification.

The certified schemes (ISO 14001 and EMAS) were primarily designed for larger manufacturing organisations. In general, SMEs have found difficulty in complying with these systems, not least because they usually do not have specialist environmental staff. An additional difficulty, especially for smaller operations, is the cost of several thousand pounds for international certification, followed by an annual cost for subsequent verification.

11.1.2 Introduction of BS 8555

In July 2003, BSI recognised that ISO 14001 was less than ideal for small businesses and introduced BS 8555. This standard is effectively the same as the original BS 7750 but has been divided into six phases; businesses can gain certification against each phase, as appropriate to their needs.

Another step being taken by BSI is the development of guidelines as to how quality, environmental and health and safety systems might be integrated in order to produce a more efficient, and less bureaucratic, process.

An over-reliance on bureaucracy is one of the criticisms of management systems; where such bureaucracy does not (obviously or immediately) result in business benefits for the organisation, it is hardly surprising that there is some scepticism about their value.

Originally intended to allow organisations to manage their environmental performance better, an EMS is increasingly being used as a marker by large customers to indicate the environmental performance of their suppliers; this has resulted in many SMEs having to implement an EMS, many of which are doing so for these marketing reasons rather than for the purer objective of environmental improvement. However, the BS 8555 standard is potentially a useful mechanism to assist businesses in this. This chapter covers EMS in general rather than any particular certification scheme. There are contacts at the end of this chapter, where further information about the individual certification schemes can be obtained.

11.1.3 Risk management

Risk *management* and risk *assessment* are beginning to be used as techniques by larger companies and are likely to become more common. Risk management as applied to environmental performance is becoming well established and this will become more refined and more broadly applicable in the future. See – and use – the risk management form in Chapter 14.

11.2 An EMS in detail

11.2.1 Costs and benefits of an EMS

Costs

- Staff time, to establish and maintain
- Need for staff training
- Audit and certification costs.

Benefits

- Identifies the potential savings from different areas of work
- Highlights areas which cause greatest environmental damage
- Attractive to new customers and major clients
- Management control
- Less examination from regulators
- Appeals to many staff
- Helps ensure legislative compliance
- Better-trained staff.

11.2.2 Some key aspects of an EMS

Organisations implement an environmental management system for several different reasons:

- They have been asked (or required) to establish such a system by their main client or customer

- Several of their competitors have established an EMS and have benefited from so doing

- There are one or two key senior staff who recognise the value of implementing an EMS for environmental, business and even ethical reasons

- They need to implement an Integrated Pollution Prevention and Control (IPPC) scheme or other legislative control, and an EMS helps with this.

For those organisations which have developed an EMS only because they have been asked or required to, there is the risk that the system will be implemented superficially. It will be seen as a paper exercise and a burden; many of the benefits which could arise are never realised.

Those organisations which implement an EMS because they genuinely wish to improve the performance of their organisation will generally be more successful – in the involvement of other staff, in the way the system is set up and in what the organisation gets out of the process.

11.2.3 Keys to success of an EMS

For those organisations which have already established a quality management system, an EMS appears a sensible next step; there appear to be many similarities between the two systems and they can be integrated. For those organisations which have not established a management system, a full EMS can be somewhat daunting – but the staged approach of BS 8555 is more attractive.

However, for any organisation which does wish to implement either a full or partial EMS there are several key issues that should be addressed.

- **Prioritise the environment as a company concern:** recognise environmental management in the organisation as important as marketing, quality, health and safety, staff management, financial management and other aspects of the organisation's performance

- **Demonstrate real senior management commitment:** the organisation needs to show that not only are the board committed to environmental management, but that senior management are demonstrating that commitment. It is also important to recognise that commitment is not just verbal or written; commitment also means that the organisation is prepared to invest money and time in changes and developments in order to bring about the environmental improvements

- **Organise a team:** the role of staff within the organisation is vital to success in achieving overall environmental improvement. This is important because staff actions can make a considerable difference to activities; staff know the details of how processes operate – and frequently know about the different options which might be more environmentally more sound. The staff who are interested and aware should be encouraged to form a 'green team' in order to keep the process of environmental improvement going forward

- **Adopt an organisation-wide strategy:** environmental performance affects all departments of an organisation, from marketing to production, transport to finance. There is nothing that does an organisation with an environmental policy more disservice than to have it pointed out that certain activities elsewhere lack environmental credibility: the commonest example is not printing marketing materials on recycled or environmentally sound paper

- **Identify investment:** apart from the cost of implementing an EMS itself, the system is likely to identify where improvements can be achieved. Investment in improved technology and better processes will result in financial and environmental gains. Costs are likely to include staff and employee time, training, some consulting assistance, materials and, possibly, equipment or materials

- **Adopt a problem-solving approach:** identify problems and then examine their possible solutions, so that gains can be made. The initial problems to be tackled should either be those that are the *easiest* to reconcile or those that have the *greatest environmental impact*. Accompanying this problem-solving approach should be the adoption of a research-orientated strategy: look at the environmental issues faced by the organisation and set up investigations into alternatives. This is an ongoing process and changes with time as new knowledge and developments are identified, so files of information should be built up about different issues

- **Recognise that an EMS requires continual improvement:** this means that each year at least one of the objectives for improvement must be better than the year before. Tackle the obvious and easiest issues first, while putting other topics into the 'research' category

- **Make it simple:** an EMS is intended to be operated throughout the organisation and therefore it should be understandable and capable of being operated by everyone in the organisation

- **Get employee ownership:** employees need to be involved and valued as part of the overall environmental improvement process. They have considerable knowledge of environmental, health and safety and related issues, especially how they relate to the work they undertake.

It is also important to train your employees using a variety of techniques to maintain their involvement and to be aware of changing procedures

- **Build in flexibility:** make the system one which works and responds to needs and changes over time. The system also needs to reflect the realities of your business, both in its activities and constraints. This also means that as time goes on the EMS should develop and evolve.

11.2.4 Generalised diagram of an EMS

Once a policy has been developed, adopted and implemented, it should be continuously reviewed and improved. The cycle is then repeated, with improvements in environmental performance being apparent each period. Note that the 'period' could be any period of time – probably a year, but in many industries it is likely that external change may well dictate a more frequent review of any environment policy.

11.3 Implementing an EMS

The steps set out below outline the different steps involved in setting up and running an environmental management system. These are not meant to be definitive, and further information and details about establishing an EMS should be obtained.

11.3.1 Management commitment

The first step for an EMS is gain top management's commitment. Management must understand the benefits of an EMS and what it will take to put an EMS in place. Management commitment and vision should be clear and communicated across the organization. Commitment also implies evidence of investment in environmental improvements.

> **Evidence:** it should be demonstrated by board meeting minutes, and senior management meeting minutes as well as by allocated budget and staff appointments.

11.3.2 Environmental aspects

Identify environmental attributes of your products, activities and services. Determine those that could have significant impacts on the environment, whether they are positive or negative.

> **Evidence:** an environmental review report setting out qualitative or quantitative issues. An example of an environmental review is provided in Chapter 10.

11.3.3 Environmental policy

Develop a statement of your organisation's commitment to the environment. Use this policy as a framework for planning and action. See Chapter 10 for examples.

> **Evidence:** the policy statement is signed and dated and is subject to regular review.

11.3.4 Structure and responsibility

Establish roles and responsibilities and provide resources. This means a 'green team' who can communicate ideas and information to and from their departmental area. It also expects that one person should be appointed as the 'environmental champion'. This would normally be a person in a middle or senior management position, and with a knowledge of systems management and/or environmental issues. In addition to internal staff, consideration should be given to involving contractors and possibly suppliers within this team.

> **Evidence:** an organisation chart with staff roles in respect of the EMS identified. Also a job description for the environmental champion.

11.3.5 Legal and other requirements

Organisations need to identify and ensure access to relevant laws and regulations. A list of all the legislation that applies to your organisation and its products and services is needed and this should be kept where appropriate staff can refer to it.

Evidence: a file or manual which keeps relevant details of legislation, regulations and directives as well as industry guidelines.

11.3.6 Training, awareness and competence

Ensure that your employees are trained and capable of carrying out their environmental responsibilities. This should combine training sessions as well as information and reminders. It is important to remember that this is a continuous process and treating it as a 'one off' would not be sufficient.

Evidence: a chart showing the training records of all staff.

11.3.7 Objectives and targets

Establish environmental goals for your organization, in line with your policy, environmental impacts, views of interested parties and other factors.

Evidence: a chart providing a summary of objectives and targets.

11.3.8 Environmental management programme

This needs the organisation to develop a plan of action to achieve objectives and targets which can lead to environmental improvement. Remember, it is not necessary to try to improve everything all at once; it should be the aim to create steady, continuous improvements which address a prioritised approach. It is also appropriate, as part of the improvement objectives, to identify the research that needs to be carried out identifying better options to current practices.

Evidence: a chart setting out the objectives, targets, schedules and indicators of success; should be reviewed and completed annually to demonstrate when actions have and haven't been successful.

11.3.9 The management system

This part of the EMS is very similar to parts of the quality management system and can, in many areas, be integrated with it. It contains a series of management steps which are set out below and which will contain the evidence identified above as well as controlling the whole system.

Evidence:

■ EMS documentation: maintain information on the EMS and related documents

- Document control: ensure effective management of procedures and other system documents
- Operational control: identify, plan and manage operations and activities in line with your environmental policy, objectives and targets
- Emergency preparedness and response: identify potential emergencies and develop procedures for preventing and responding to them
- Monitoring and measurement: monitor key activities and track performance, in particular. This needs to be done for those activities where objectives and targets are set as well as for activities where a baseline for future improvements is needed
- Non-conformance and corrective and preventive action: identify and correct problems and prevent recurrences
- Records: keep adequate records of EMS performance
- EMS audit: periodically verify that your EMS is operating as intended
- Management review: periodically review your EMS with an eye to continual improvement.

11.3.10 Communication

Establish processes for internal and external communications on environmental management issues. This is important for your staff as well as your customers and your suppliers.

Evidence: many companies produce an annual report which can set out their policy and the achievements they have made in implementing that policy. Alternatively it could be part of the larger company annual report. It does not have to be extensive or posh; some of the most interesting reports have been short four-page leaflets.

11.4 Template for implementing environmental management

Set out over the next few pages is a template to help your organisation set up the first, most important, steps of an EMS. Not all the sections will be relevant to your organisation. Delete or ignore sections which do not apply to you and set out the remainder in a clear format, on your organisation's headed paper and with relevant details to 'personalise' the template to your business. Alter as necessary. The document itself is not intended to be a manual, but its content may contribute towards producing one.

There are several benefits to your doing this:

- Increasingly, customers and clients want to see your policy and other details

- It will encourage you to think carefully about your environmental policy

- It will help your staff to contribute to environmental implementation in your business

- It can be recorded, logged and filed for future reference and for new staff.

This document may be combined with your quality management or your health and safety system; it is up to you to ensure there is no contradiction between the systems.

Any sentences in italics are intended as brief explanatory notes for you and should be deleted before the final document is produced. The aim of this is to give you a framework that can be used to build from. All elements are useful but in a very small company some of the information could not be used or implemented.

11

Template for implementing environmental management

ABC Ltd

1. Company structure

organisation chart

2. Management responsibilities

The implementation of our environmental policy at ABC Ltd is being followed in a considered and coordinated way.

.... (name) has overall management responsibility for the environmental policy throughout the company.

Environmental policy area	Name/Position/Responsibility
Legislation and compliance	
Maintenance and emissions control	
Waste and recycling control	
Transport and discharges	
All other environmental matters	
Packaging	

3. Environmental policy
Environmental Policy Statement
Doc No: Revision   Date:

Authorised by:

At ABC we have a responsibility to the environment. Activities are regularly evaluated and environmental concerns are addressed with a view to selecting the best practicable environmental option.

The environmental policy has the following principles: *(insert your text as necessary)*

Regulations and legislation

Resources

Energy

Transport

Discharges and emissions

Packaging

Waste

Organisation

Communication

This policy will be made available to staff, suppliers, customers and any other person who might be interested.

Suppliers
We will work with our suppliers to ensure the highest quality of product is used and that information on types and strains of products are fully declared.

Signed: Position: Date:

4. Setting objectives

ABC Ltd recognises two types of objective:
- Improvement: moving forward
- Maintenance: keeping up a high standard of performance

A step-by-step approach to setting up environmental objectives has been carried out:

1. Environmental aspects of policy have been considered
2. Environmental legal issues have been addressed
3. Priority issues have been set
4. Existing performance levels with regards to the important environmental aspects and legal drivers have been assessed
5. Improvement objectives as appropriate **AND/OR**   maintenance objectives as appropriate have been established
6. The method of achieving the objectives has been set out.

Setting up objectives

Improvement objectives

Improvement objectives	Who	When	How
To reduce energy usage per tonne of product by 2% based on 2004 usage		End 2005	Energy efficiency drives, Lighting controls and optimisation of throughput
To provide environmental training for all staff where appropriate to environmental improvement		End 2005	Training packs, and coaching. Funding being sought
To reduce packaging		Ongoing	Reconfigure bags to use less material
To improve drainage and discharge controls		Summer 2005	Initial mapping to identify issues
To increase range of resources, materials and equipment from recycled or environmentally sound sources		Ongoing	Continue to seek recycled alternatives to present materials
To increase range of materials recycled.		Ongoing	Continue to segregate and monitor
To formulate and implement an environmentally sensitive purchasing regime		End of 2007	Decide performance criteria with suppliers, implement purchasing regime using tools such as periodic supplier reporting and audit
Integrated Pollution Prevention and Control compliance		March 2005	Work with CESMB to complete application
Spill kit availability		January 2005	Purchase and include training

Maintenance objectives	Method of achievement
To maintain continual compliance with IPPC regulations	Compliance with existing factory operating procedures and criteria; maintenance of site cleanliness; efficient working and maintenance of filters and materials protection, its instrumentation and hardware; constant monitoring, auditing or inspection
To adhere to sector guidelines	Regular checks on website, circulars and conferences
Maintain transport efficiency and considerations	Regular maintenance and selection of correct vehicle for correct load and journey
Continue segregating recyclate	Monitor performance and liaise with waste/recycling contractor
Monitor compliance with relevant legislation	Audit and check process and equipment on regular appropriate basis
Maintain awareness of new legislation and its implications	Visit Netregs site annually
Improve fuel monitoring	Monitor and record
Optimise load carrying and care in selection of new vehicles	Match load and vehicle and journey

Management of objectives

The objectives set out above and in future years will be discussed and agreed at the Senior Management meeting in January each year.

The agreed objectives and targets are then applied to each department's aims and objectives.

11

5. Training

Staff training register

Name	Position	Training type/ Course	Course title	Date/duration	Course provider	Location	Level of training*

*CPD Certificate and/or level of training

6. Reporting

Environmental reporting

Environmental objectives	Targets achieved 2004	Achievements/outcomes/benefits	Cost	Savings	Target for year 2005

Examples

Reduce energy use per tonne by 2%
Environmental training
Reduce packaging
Improve drainage
Increase use of recycled materials
Increase recycling
Environmental purchasing
IPPC compliance
Spill kits and training

7. Additional Information

Suppliers

Supply Chain: Environmental criteria in relation to supplier selection.

ABC Ltd has introduced environmental criteria into the supplier selection process. Furthermore, we have developed an Environmental Purchasing Policy to ensure that goods and services purchased for the company are manufactured, delivered, used and managed at end-of-life in an environmentally responsible manner.

ABC Ltd now expects its suppliers to show evidence of their commitment to the environment by having an environmental policy.

Waste
The overall responsibility for waste collection and management within ABC Ltd lies with .... (Director).

The current waste contractor for ABC Ltd is .... (company name); their Waste Licence number is: ....

ABC Ltd does not produce any hazardous or special waste.

ABC Ltd will regularly scrutinise waste disposal and waste management processes to ensure that all controlled wastes are handled in a careful and environmentally appropriate manner.

Communications
ABC Ltd communicates openly about activities and prepares an annual report which addresses environmental policy performance and the achievement of policy objectives for the company.

Copies of ABC Ltd's annual report are available from Head Office to all our customers, employees and other stakeholders (partners, suppliers, contractors, and community group).

11

11.5 Sources of information

British Standards Institute

Information on management systems.
www.bsi-global.com

Institute of Ecology and Environmental Management

Professional body which represents and
supports professionals in the fields of ecology
and environmental management.
www.ieem.org.uk

Institute of Environmental Management and Assessment

Leading organisation for environmental
management.
www.iema.net

International Network for Environmental Management

Useful site for more information and help.
www.inem.org

Nokia

Interesting site with lots of detail, not just
about EMS. Follow links to 'About Nokia' and
then to 'Corporate responsibility'.
www.nokia.co.uk

Developing your staff

Case study

A small manufacturer of car parts, based in Waltham Cross, Hertfordshire, was required by its main client to implement an ISO 14001 Environmental Management System.

As part of this process, CESMB also provided the company with a thorough environmental training programme for all the management and supervisory staff, and other information for manual staff. The training raised awareness of the environmental issues facing the company, why it was implementing an EMS, the role the staff played in that and what was expected of them. An interesting development was the number of staff who were very positive towards the environment and only too willing and pleased to do their bit.

12

12.1 Overview

One of the biggest issues facing any organisation that wishes to make changes is how best to help, encourage, or require the staff to work to the new systems.

None of us likes change – at worst, we see it as a threat to jobs and security; at best, an annoyance. Unless something is clearly 'wrong', most of us prefer to keep things as they are: *'if it ain't broke, don't fix it!'*. Changing work routines or approaches in response to environmental improvement is no different to making any other change, so careful and sensitive handling of the introduction of the changes, and the communication of them, is required.

More positively, many people have a very sound perspective of the environment: we recognise that our health and welfare is closely linked to a healthy environment and, where we can see that we will benefit from helping to improve the environment, we are usually willing to change. A good example of this occurred a few years ago, when many people changed from using underarm sprays containing chlorofluorocarbons (CFCs) to those without. The recognition that an increased use of CFCs was damaging the ozone layer (and might result in increases in skin cancer) prompted many people to use more environmentally sound body sprays.

Many of the organisational changes needed to help improve environmental performance will, however, be more radical, and will involve changes in the way staff work. Any organisation wanting to reduce waste and energy costs can install a wide range of technical equipment – but even greater savings will be made if staff are correctly trained in the use of the new equipment. Most organisations can probably save about 10% of their energy costs simply by getting their staff to switch off equipment when they have finished with it, and by other 'no-cost' adjustments to heating and lighting controls. Businesses considering recycling require staff to separate wastes into different types rather than just throw it into one large container.

But the change in staff thinking and approach to their work goes far beyond these steps; it requires:

- **Purchasing staff** to consider the environmental criteria of purchases
- **Finance staff** to carry out a comprehensive cost/benefit analysis when making investment decisions
- **Marketing staff** to understand the environmental qualities of the products and services provided by the organisation.

12

Involving and encouraging the staff into these sorts of changes is a slow, long-term and potentially difficult job. It will not be accomplished solely by sending everyone on a one-day training course, nor by sending two or three managers on a week-long training course; nor will it be achieved by buying in some environmental training manuals or CDs.

In reality, it will involve all of these steps and more to establish a holistic and ongoing process. It will also mean that the outcome of the training, the new skills for environmental improvement, will need to be monitored and assessed. However, training comes in many forms; reminders to staff of new practices and approaches is critical. These reminders can be achieved by the use of stickers by light switches; internal email reminders to switch off computers at the end of the day; posters which remind staff of particular issues. These devices all have a part to play in building on, and reinforcing, the new knowledge and skills.

12.2 Environmental training: the context

Environmental training is frequently seen as a 'bolt-on extra' that figures marginally in any training programme for one or, possibly, two years – and then is considered to be 'job done'.

Effective environmental training should be continuous and varied; it should be targeted and have a practical approach, that helps organisations implement environmental improvements efficiently and comprehensively.

12.2.1 Training principles

In order to spread the environmental skills, knowledge and action throughout an organisation, a process similar to the management of change needs to be applied. This can be viewed as having five stages of information flow:

- Awareness of the information, the subject or the topic
- Acquisition of further or more detailed information
- Assessment and analysis of the information
- Acting upon the information
- Monitoring and evaluation of the change derived from the information.

The key factors which are generally recognised as being essential to an effective training programme can be applied to environmental training, as much as any other training programme:

- Start from where the learners are: in other words, do not use high-level environmental terms and concepts that participants are not familiar with

- Relate environmental information, concepts and ideas to participants' own work and personal life

- Use a mix of information, assimilation and application of the environmental concepts

- Include a strong practical element to the training: remember the old Chinese proverb: 'I hear and I forget, I see and I know, I do and I understand'

- Build a strong link between environmental understanding and the work of, and benefits to, the organisation

- Provide a template for ongoing development and application of environmental understanding and skills in the workplace.

- Integrate environmental understanding and applications with management and other training; encourage personal reflection

- Provide a sound basis for improved decision making.

12.2.2 Relating environmental training to management responsibilities

Any organisation which takes a holistic approach to its environmental improvement will have different managers performing different environmental roles. The chart on the next two pages shows the relationship between areas of general management responsibility and the related aspects of environmental responsibility, and the training topics which should be considered for each area. There is also a cross-reference to the various chapters of this manual.

12

Management area	Environmental aspects/responsibility	Environmental training topics	Chapter ref
Marketing / public relations	Company environmental responsibility; Environmental qualities of products or services; Environmental qualities of competitors or environmental leaders; Whole-life costs and LCA; Community and public authority liaison	Life cycle analysis Environmental marketing Environmental communication	Chapter 8
Production	Resource consumption issues; Waste and energy consumption; Machine efficiency; Environmental impacts of emissions and discharges and their monitoring and control.	Environmental recording techniques and equipment Pollution impacts Company-specific product impacts	Chapter 6
Purchasing	Supplier environmental performance; Product and service environmental criteria; Whole-life costs and LCA; Ethical issues	Life cycle analysis Supplier assessment Comparative product analysis BPEO	Chapter 8
Human resources	Inclusion of environmental responsibilities in staff job descriptions; Environment as part of appraisal process Environmental training for managers and staff	Environmental training needs analysis, integrated environmental management training	Chapter 12
Quality/H&S	Environmental risk assessment; Management and operational control; Systems management; Integration of environment with H&S and quality; Environmental impact assessment	Management systems and integration EIA	Chapters 10, 11

Management area	Environmental aspects/responsibility	Environmental training topics	Chapter ref
Distribution/transport	Fleet management; Reverse logistics Packaging management and recycling New fuels and improved vehicle performance	Waste management Transport option and driver training; New technologies	Chapters 4, 5
Communications/IT	Publication of policies; Equipment management Raising staff awareness of policies and practices	Environmental communications, policy development	Chapters 11, 12
Finance	Investment in new technologies; Identifying savings for re-investment; Whole life costings	Green accounting, cost-benefit analysis. LCA	Chapter 9
Facilities	Energy management; Environmental techniques in buildings maintenance; New building techniques and environmental considerations	Energy, Green Buildings management; New clean techniques and technologies	Chapters 5, 9
Senior management	All of the above in broad outline together with understanding legal implications associated with the business and the need for integration and commitment	LCA; BPEO Legislation policy implementation	Chapters 2, 7, 11
Staff	Specific environmental aspects of work	Environmental aspects of jobs, as applicable	

12

12.2.3 Supporting staff environmental development

Too often, training is seen as a simple cure for the organisation's problems and difficulties. The assumption, too often, is that providing staff with training will help them do their jobs better. For the staff themselves, the perception is often that training, although it might be interesting, is probably a pleasant day away from their normal work; if it is of some use in the future, well, that is a bonus. This is of course a gross generalisation; and there are many employers who do approach training in a well-organised, objective and well-supported manner. However, there are many who adopt the 'training will be useful' approach and do little to identify, assess or support their trainees.

There also appears to have been little analysis of the training carried out aside from the initial response forms completed at the end of the course, often referred to as 'happy sheets'. What the happy sheet does is to indicate the quality of delivery of the training session, the appeal of the presenter and the quality of the accommodation and food; what it does *not* do is to indicate the long-term effectiveness of the training and how it has benefited both the participant and their employer.

Training needs to be supported by a range of other strategies from the organisation. For environmental management training and development this is especially important because, for many organisations, it is moving into a new area of skill and knowledge – and, indeed, a new area of organisational strategy. The diagram below shows the cultural issues which need to be considered if organisations are to effectively support the environmental development of staff – or, indeed, *any* development.

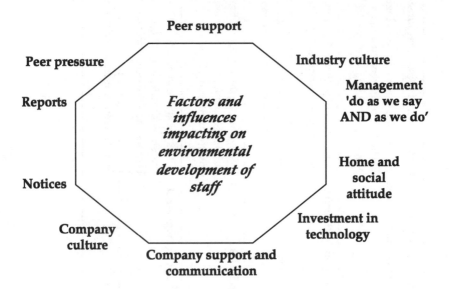

In some instances a 'cart and horse' syndrome exists: is it better to train staff in the environmental area, and *then* build up the support mechanisms to maximise effective benefit from that training – or is it more appropriate to develop the support strategy to effectively support staff prior to them undertaking the environmental training?

In reality, it is probably a bit of both: you are advised to initially train a small group of key staff, including at least one senior manager; they can then establish a support strategy, such that environmental training for the remaining staff will be effectively supported.

12.2.4 Company support and communication

Given that environmental training aims to change participants' attitudes and behaviour – both in their workplace and their home life – there is the need for constant reminders and ongoing information updating to help employees maintain their new behaviours and attitudes. With the advent of electronic systems in the workplace, communicating with staff can be varied and innovative; some suggestions are listed below:

- **Green column in company newsletter:** many companies produce a small newsletter, or a more formal annual report. Having a regular environmental article within such publications will help maintain both internal and external environmental awareness of what the company is doing

- **Green awards for best suggestions or good practice**: this is quite common practice; where the awards can be related to company savings, they can be self-funding. If such a scheme is being set up, staff need to know the criteria against which suggestions are being judged – and the likely rewards

> **Case study: Awards**
> A national company, with several small manufacturing plants, specialises in the manufacture of a range of metallic products. A member of staff suggested a modification to the process which would reduce significantly the level of water consumption. The saving for the company amounted to about £10,000 per year and the member of staff received a 10% reward.

- **Posters for offices and workstations:** notices adjacent to light switches to remind staff to turn them off, posters above electrical equipment and other notices about collection of waste are a useful means of reminding staff of the importance of good practice. However, they do need to be regularly renewed – partly to keep them looking smart but also to keep staff reading them to reinforce the message

- **Email messages to staff as reminders:** the high use of emails and electronic communications in the workplace provide another avenue for transmitting messages to staff, and any company with a computer

12

network can easily arrange for regular messages to be sent to staff with reminders for different actions such as turning off equipment. A request not to print off email messages (and thus waste paper) unless necessary is now reasonably common

■ **'Log-off' message on computer screen when shutting down:** such as a reminder to turn off all adjacent equipment and lights etc. This is a variation on the electronic messaging

■ **Withdrawal of previous facilities:** where organisations are trying to change long-established habits of staff, some radical steps may need to be taken, such as removing the facilities that were previously used and forcing staff to adopt the new practices.

> **Case study: If persuasion fails ...**
> A multinational company, with a large office-based operation, tried to introduce a recycling regime a few years ago, after it had identified that collecting paper and metal drinks cans would be beneficial. It placed clearly marked bins in each office area, coupled with a vigorous publicity programme. However, after a month or so, the level of paper and cans collected was miserly. It was noticed that, after the initial burst, staff had simply reverted to their former habits of putting waste in their own personal bin by their desk. The company therefore removed all personal waste bins, with each office area having only one waste collection point – with clearly marked bins for the different wastes. The scheme became an overnight success.

The essence of these communications is the need to continually update information, raise new issues and cause employees to stop and think about their actions.

12.2.5 Integrated approach to environmental training

Having pointed out the fact that the environment needs to be seen as an integral and important aspect of the overall organisational strategy, and that environmental training needs to avoid being a bolt-on activity for the organisation, it is worthwhile seeing how environmental training can be most effectively combined with other training activities. Not only would such an approach be effective as a means of learning (because participants will be more able to relate the environmental training to their other job training) but it is more cost-effective in both staff time and cost. There are three main approaches which may be adopted in order to achieve this integration:

■ Take an existing environmental training activity and change the focus to include a management skill development

■ Develop an entirely new training activity, which has both specialist and environmental outcomes

■ Integrate an environmental training activity within the programme of activities for other objectives.

There are difficulties with all these approaches, especially as – to be really effective – trainers should have environmental knowledge themselves, as well as expertise in their normal training areas.   However, this is not insurmountable and is an objective that organisations could strive towards.

12.3 Staff development

12.3.1 Environmental training needs analysis (ETNA)

In the previous section, the needs of different managers and staff for a different focus for their environmental training was set out. In order to bring this about it is, therefore, logical that organisations should employ a sound method to identify what environmental training is needed by different managers and staff.

Each organisation will need to develop a flexible and ongoing strategy, covering a range of different issues and methods. The aim of this section is to suggest what an environmental training needs analysis looks like and how it may be applied.

The objectives of an ETNA are to assess training required to achieve:

■ Development of environmental awareness and commitment for all

■ Creation of appropriate environmental understanding and skills among both specialist and strategic managers

■ Establishment of environmental understanding and relevant technical skills for operators

■ Creation of commitment and environmental understanding from senior executives.

Any organisation needs to address environmental training by considering three discrete needs:

■ The overall needs of the **organisation**

■ The needs of **managerial and operative staff**

■ The needs of **specialist staff** – this means not just the environmental coordinator, but also staff with specific environmentally related jobs, such as waste control and health and safety.

12

Overleaf is a sample ETNA form, used to assess overall training needs within the organisation, which could be developed to include specific environmental-related or job-related topics and questions. The form is a simple, quick and reasonably indicative means of identifying training needs, either on an organisational or individual basis.

Environmental training needs analysis

Overall organisation needs

Organisation name:

Main activities (manufacturing/services and description):

Size/Number of employees:

How does the organisation currently impact on the environment?
For each topic in the table below describe how that impact occurs. If you
believe that the organisation has no impact on that feature of the environment,
explain why.   Some features have been included in the table and, in the first
case, an example is provided.

This should also include positive impacts on the environment so that where an
organisation undertakes work which enhances the environment this should be
noted.

Environmental feature	Type of impact	Cause of impact or reason for no impact	
Air	*Carbon dioxide*	*Burning oil, gas, for heating and lighting. Transport*	
Water			
Land			
Resources			
Waste			
Nuisance (noise, smells, visual)			
Habitats/wildlife			
Transport			
Site issues			
Indirect (via suppliers or customers)			
Other (state)			
Other (state)			

Does the organisation have an environmental policy?

What are the main features of the environmental policy?

What environmental legislation impacts upon the company – e.g. waste, emissions and discharges, packaging etc?

What do customers expect of the environmental performance of the organisation – that is, has the organisation been asked about its environmental performance by any customers or clients?

What are the significant environmental costs of the organisation – e.g. is waste disposal significant, energy costs high? Costs of complying with discharge or emission limits?

How will environmental progress be monitored?

Considering these last three questions, do your responses indicate the need for particular environmental training for staff?

What environmental training is currently offered by the organisation to its staff?

Has this environmental training been:
- one-off?
- separate from other training?
- linked to any other training?
- repeated?
- included in any induction training?

How can environmental training be integrated with the other training?

How are environmental messages communicated from the organisation to managers and staff? How continuous is this?

What other environmental communication techniques will be used to support the environmental training?

12

12.3.2 An environmental training programme for your business

Raising staff awareness of environmental issues can best be delivered by a training programme which is then supported by a range of other environmental communication strategies.

Set out below is a sample of a training programme which could be delivered within one day. It tries to mix both theoretical and practical learning and relate that to the business activities.

Sample environmental training programme

Duration: about 6 hours

Suitable group size: 10-25 people

Venue: Training room with flip chart, slide projection facilities etc. This should ideally be on the business site so that visits can be made to study particular areas and their environmental issues.

Objectives
The programme will:

- Separate environmental myth from environmental fact

- Relate environmental issues to the activities of your business

- Identify steps that can be taken immediately to save money and benefit the environment

- Consider future steps to build environmental improvements into the company strategy

- Encourage groups of staff to work together and share information and experiences.

Programme

Session 1
15 minutes

Introduction and outline of the programme: this session will set out the purpose of the training and place it within the overall strategy of the company. Ideally this session would be delivered by a member of senior management.

Session 2
45 minutes

Environmental issues – the global, national and local aspects: this will provide some pertinent facts about the environmental issues such as global climate change, pollution, waste and resource consumption. The session should also relate each issue to personal and organisational performance and pressures.

Session 3
45 minutes

Environmental issues and your business: talk and discussion, which will include legislation, financial controls and prioritising environmental improvement; detailed consideration of the direction that legislation is taking, the pressures on businesses and the increasing costs that businesses are incurring.
This should be followed by a group discussion to identify particular concerns for your company.

Session 4
45 minutes

Life cycle analysis: a practical group activity to demonstrate the environmental impacts of a product. This is a very successful and enlightening group activity which looks at all the environmental issues associated with two particular alternative products. Typical examples might include a china mug and a disposable mug (see case study in Chapter 7) or a disposable ballpoint pen and a refillable pen. For a particular company, it may be appropriate to select company products.
It is best carried out with the products in front of participants and using flip chart and felt pens.

Session 5
30 minutes

Group discussion and developing an environmental improvement action plan: if you had to reduce this programme to a half-day, then this could be the final session; it would encourage participants to identify priorities for the company and discuss how a 'green team' could be established to move improvements forward.

12

Session 6 *90 minutes*	**Saving money the environmental way**: carrying out a waste audit, identifying priorities and actions – a talk followed by practical group session. This is a very practical session and involves looking at all the different activities in the organisation and the wastes that are produced. It should follow the waste hierarchy approach and use the tables and activities set out in Chapter 3.
Session 7 *45 minutes*	**Future trends:** getting ahead of the competition, what laws, financial controls and pressures are likely to affect your business in the next three years. This session involves some forward planning and considers the changes that are known to be happening and others that can be predicted. It can also begin to focus on some of the objectives and targets for improvement.
Session 8 *30 minutes*	**The next steps**: involving other staff in the team, making changes and where they can lead. A group discussion about how to achieve the targets and objectives set out in the previous activity.
Session 9 *15 minutes*	Closing remarks, questions and discussions.

Such a programme would be supported by a handbook and supporting notes. In addition, back-up material providing sources of further information should be provided.

A programme such as this would do a reasonable job in providing participants with a sound understanding of the environment and how it relates to their work and their organisation.

However, as a stand-alone, one-day, programme it has shortcomings:

■ It is only one day and there is no provision for further development

■ It is entirely focused on environmental training and does not attempt to integrate this with other skills

■ It offers no qualification or credit, which could be used as an incentive for further work and study

■ If offered *outside* the organisation, it may not be effective at training a team within an organisation; it trains one individual who is then reliant upon the organisation itself to build on the trained understanding and skills.

A CD-ROM containing PowerPoint slides detailing all of the sessions outlined above will shortly be available from the publishers.

12.3.3   Overall considerations

In developing staff to increase their environmental awareness and knowledge, and apply that awareness to achieve better environmental performance in the organisation, there is a careful balance to be struck. On the one hand, it is important for *all* staff to have a basic level of environmental awareness, to be able to apply the principles to their work and to understand, when changes are introduced, the rationale behind those changes. On the other hand, in order to really drive forward the desired changes, it is important to have a recognised champion in the organisation, as well as a team of people who can make a real contribution to progress.

There is a strong similarity between the organisational approach set out above and the approach recommended for implementing health and safety; it is, therefore, not surprising that many companies double-up their health and safety and their environmental teams and, in many instances, incorporate quality management as well.

12.4 Sources of information

Centre for Environment and Safety Management for Business

Range of training programmes from half day to a year, designed to ensure that businesses benefit from environmental improvement.
www.mdx.ac.uk/www/cesmb

Centre for Sustainable Environmental Management

High-level training for businesses.
www.csem.org.uk

Egeneration   Based in south-east England, but with lots of general information.
www.egeneration.co.uk

LANTRA   Practical skills for environmental and land-based sectors.
www.lantra.co.uk

Middlesex University Press

Publishers of this book, and also the CD of training materials referred to earlier.
www.mupress.co.uk

Stewart Anthony   Training and consultancy. Email contact at:
stewart55anthony@hotmail.com

12

See also section 6.4, 'Sources of information'.

Future trends

Case study

A car repair company in north London needed, in the early 1990s, to buy some new paint spray equipment. The owners had a choice of two pieces of equipment: the lower-cost version was adequate for the work and complied with the existing legislation, whereas the more expensive equipment went some way beyond the requirements of current legislation. They decided to purchase the less expensive equipment.

After about four years, legislation was tightened – but the equipment did not perform to the new legal limits. The company now needed to buy the updated version of the more expensive equipment. Businesses must be aware of changing legislation and plan investments and developments which will keep their operations performing legally.

13

13.1 Overview

In terms of its impact on business operations, the environment has been an increasing concern since the mid-1980s. Before this time there were significant events: London smogs, oil tanker spills, DDT and other pesticide pollutants, concerns about acid rain. However, each of these events was generally seen in isolation; politicians, business leaders and others outside the environmental field tended to treat each incident as a separate problem.

For businesses in the UK, the 1980s marked a considerable move towards the concept of quality. However, 'the environment' was not considered to be an element of 'quality' in most of the strategies adopted by larger businesses. But there was a growing expectation of a better quality of life – and with this came the expectation of a better environment in which to live.

13.1.1 Conference on the Environment

In 1992, at the United Nations *Conference on the Environment* in Rio de Janeiro, many of these concerns were pulled together and an agenda and targets for future environmental protection were set out.

Even before the Rio conference, the European Union had been setting out a wide spectrum of legislation, to control an increasing range of materials and activities. This trend in legislation has continued – and indeed increased – into the new millennium. As new research showed the damaging impacts on the environment and human health of ever-smaller quantities of chemicals and processes, so the legislation, driven from Europe, has expanded and extended its scope.

But the Rio conference also introduced the concept of 'sustainable development', an approach which recognised the triple importance of environmental, social and financial sustainability. Along with major national and multinational companies, many organisations started to consider their own response to sustainable development, and began to examine their own supply chains – which, of course, put pressure upon those businesses within the supply chains. Not only did this cause these smaller businesses to consider the environment in relation to their business but, where companies sourced materials from overseas, similar requirements were applied, causing the overseas suppliers to respond to these environmental supply chain pressures.

13.1.2 Ethical investment

Another significant development in the late nineties and beyond was the growing interest in 'ethical investment'. This avoids channelling investment funds into companies that operate in certain sectors, such as

13

tobacco, arms, or those companies (or even countries) with poor records in employment, environmental issues, human rights or health and safety.

In 2002, the UK Government identified that the two most important environmental issues which would face the country in the coming decade were *waste* and *energy*. The production of waste (and especially its disposal to landfill) and the consumption of energy, both have to be reduced; businesses are seen as an obvious target for achieving this. In the next few years, therefore, it is clear that pressure on all businesses to improve their environmental performance will continue to grow. This pressure will come in a variety of ways – financial incentives, legislation, customer pressure and public concern – and those businesses that respond to these issues best (and earliest) are more likely to prosper.

13.2 Three major trends

This book has tried to offer practical advice and help to businesses by explaining:

- **Why** the environment, in all its different facets, is important to businesses

- **What** businesses and individuals can do to address these issues

- **Where** further information can be found.

Ultimately, however, it comes down to the managers and staff in each business and to *you*. Implementing some or all of these changes in your business (and, where appropriate, at home) will make a big difference to the environment your children and grandchildren live in.

You need to keep up to speed with these environmental developments, and this section considers the trends over which you need to maintain a watching brief. Use websites or journals to develop and extend your understanding of how the environment is changing and what you can do to help. We started this book with a quotation from philosopher Edmund Burke, which remains valid:

> '... no man made a greater mistake than he who did nothing because he could do so little'.

The trends for the future can be seen in terms of three core areas:

- **Legislation**
- **Business practice**
- **Social and political.**

These are now considered in greater detail.

13.2.1 The trends in legislation

In some ways, this area is the easiest to describe and predict. Some of the upcoming legislation from the EU is already known; dates for the implementation of new directives over the next five years are already set out.

In broad terms, the trends in this legislation are that it is going to cover a wider range of topics and will require more stringent standards. Some of the issues which businesses need to address in terms of likely new environmental legislation are:

- Disposal of batteries – this will be controlled

- Increasing controls on hazardous chemicals

- Encouragement to move away from solvent-based materials to water-based chemicals

- Stricter control on gases emitted to the atmosphere

- Stricter controls on liquids discharged to lakes and rivers and sea

- Increasing emphasis on reduction of materials which are disposed of as waste

- Increasing pressure to move away from artificial processes towards 'biotechnology'' techniques.

Therefore, the implication for business is that investment in new technologies, new filtration systems and new monitoring equipment needs to address higher specification, better levels of operation and finer details of monitoring.

For businesses interested in more details of forthcoming legislation, some suggested websites are listed at the end of this chapter.

13.2.2 The trends in business practice

There have been several major changes in business practices since the 1980s, when the rush to develop, purchase and supply products and services which met quality standards became widespread. This then led to other issues being included within the supply chain criteria, such as health and safety, ethical principles and environmental standards. It is generally perceived that many of these criteria are now of equal importance to the price of the goods and services provided.

It is conceivable that the next developments are likely to include closer links between the organisation and its customers and clients, so that there becomes a synergistic supply process – whereby the customer is as much involved in the supplied product and service process as the supplier.

13

The other trend in the supply of goods and services is that it will go entirely the opposite way: customers will continue to demand goods and services at ever-lower prices, the consequence of which will be lower quality, and smaller numbers of suppliers – operating with less and less overhead and with little regard for environmental impacts and other criteria.

It is clear that in some sectors of the economy this diversity into two opposite directions is already happening. In food, it is easily possible to purchase low-cost food, highly processed and with questionable nutritional and health values while, at the other end of the scale, purchasing good-quality, nutritious, often organic, food – but at a premium price.

Similarly, in tourism it is possible to opt for low-cost package holidays or for more specialist holidays, to more exotic locations, in better-quality hotels and with more consideration for the environment – albeit at a much higher price. Such tourism activity is sometimes referred to as 'responsible tourism' because it reflects the full cost of impacts on society and communities and on the environment itself.

The trend in Europe and in major multinational companies is to move towards sustainability, an approach which recognises the triple importance of people, finances and the environment. It is clear, from the two examples above, that responsible tourism and organic food are more likely to prove to be sustainable strategies than their lower-cost alternatives.

Overseas sourcing

The other clear trend which has been taking place for the past several years is the move towards sourcing products and services from overseas. Largely due to lower labour costs, goods and services procured from developing countries can out-compete on price – though health and safety, environmental and ethical concerns are less clear. Whether there will be a move to ensure that overseas suppliers perform to all the standards that are common in developed countries is debatable. Although there are many examples of overseas suppliers (and UK businesses) ignoring environmental concerns, there are increasing examples where consideration for the environment, economy and communities in supplier countries are coming to the fore; the Body Shop is perhaps a good example of this considerate and fair trade behaviour.

13.2.3 Social and political trends

This is the most uncertain to be able to predict. The pattern over the past few years is that society is tending to split into two main groups: those with a disposable income and who are willing to pay for luxuries and benefit from a 'good quality of life'; and, at the other extreme, those with very limited disposable income, working long hours for low pay.

If this pattern does continue, this would reflect the divergence suggested in the business practices just outlined.

Other patterns in society include an increasing concern with quality of food and other goods; a concern with the overall quality of the air and water; and a desire for some to develop good personal health and fitness.

The trends for the future in terms of politics and other aspects of society changes are very uncertain, possibly being driven less by environmental concerns than concern for personal security and safety.

There is one other issue which has been changing over the past few years and which will continue to change: the small, but growing, awareness that we are living on one planet – and that all peoples need to share in the wealth potential of the planet. Our failure to do this would result in those countries with higher standards being a target for people from less-developed countries to migrate to. We should also appreciate that as two very large countries, India and China, develop very rapidly (as they are doing at present), so the pressures on resources and the environment will continue to increase.

13.3 Business concerns

Extending the previous overview of business trends, we now set out a number of topics which businesses may need to be concerned about in the next two years. It should be emphasised that most of the suggestions are largely based on past and recent practices; where clear indications of future trends are known, these have been specified. The indications are set out in short statements in order to aid clarity.

The various trends include:

- **Energy**
- **Waste**
- **Transport**
- **Corporate disclosure**
- **Ethics**
- **Building design**
- **Polluter pays**
- **Civil liability**
- **Risk management**
- **Product durability**
- **Responsible tourism**
- **Media**
- **Business start up**

These are now discussed in more detail.

13

13.3.1 Energy

All the indications are that, for the UK in particular, the easy years of North Sea oil and gas are over. In 2004 we became net importers of gas for the first time for over 30 years. There are three main areas of concern for our energy supply:

- **Security of supply:** as supplies of energy are being imported from further parts of the planet, and with an increasingly disjointed security and terrorist situation, being able to ensure adequate and secure energy supplies will be very important. This is allied to the lack of investment in new power plants within the UK, which could increase our dependence on imported energy supplies

- **Alternative sources of energy and power generation:** wind generators are likely to increase in number, but are more likely to be located offshore or in other areas where they make less environmental impact. Solar panels, notably photovoltaics, are a steadily developing technology, and sources of bio- and waste-originated energy will increase in importance. Improvements in boiler efficiency and increases in combined heat and power systems are also likely to become more important.

  It should be recognised that whatever source of energy is selected, there are significant environmental impacts; all the above alternatives have arguments both for and against

- **Energy minimisation:** this will become more prevalent, partly in response to increasing energy costs and in response to the reduced availability of energy. Initially this will be more important for businesses but gradually it will become important for domestic consumers as well. In the UK, two significant price rises in 2004 are indications of increased pressure on supplies.

13.3.2 Waste

The UK will have to reduce its dependence on landfill over the next decade and send less material (and fewer types of material) to landfill. Several consequences are likely to follow:

- An increased cost for disposal of waste to landfill
- Increased pressure for recycling
- Increased demand for recycled products
- Pressure to reduce various chemicals going to landfill
- Pressure to eliminate certain products going to landfill, notably batteries and electrical and electronic goods
- Elimination of organic materials going to landfill.

Therefore, businesses involved in landfill operations need to consider diversification, and companies with an interest in recycling, waste management, re-engineering and production of goods from recycled materials may have an opportunity to develop and expand.

13.3.3 Transport

This is likely to remain an important, divisive and growing major issue. It is already important for businesses in terms of congestion and business delays; it will be of increasing importance for its impact on the environment from manufacturing processes, oil consumption, pollution and disposal of the end-of-life vehicles.

Cities are likely to follow the lead of London in establishing congestion charges in their city centres, with relief for those vehicles with non-fossil-fuel power systems.

Vehicles are more likely to be developed with improved efficiency, with greater computer and sensor control, and road charging systems.

Air transport is just beginning to face questions about the impact it makes from pollutants on the atmosphere and the extent to which existing or new airports can be developed. Whether predicted patterns of increase in air travel will be realised is uncertain but, if they are, then complaints about the environmental impact of air transport will only increase.

For businesses it would therefore be sensible to address the issues of their location, the availability of public transport, the proximity of staff and the proximity to their major customers.

13.3.4 Corporate disclosure

In the past few years, shareholders have begun to express their views to companies about various business matters. At present this is directed towards salaries of executives and financial performance, but shareholder concerns about environmental performance of companies could be part of the future.

Businesses, particularly in Europe, which establish the EMAS version of an environmental management system are required to make a disclosure about their environmental concerns, and this could extend to the UK.

The Freedom of Information Act (which came into effect in January 2005), and the shortly-to-be-validated Aarhus Convention, are designed to allow the public the right to environmental information.

13

The increasing tendency to litigation is also likely to pressurise businesses to declare their environmental performance.

13.3.5 Ethics

Ethical investment and fair trade are two indications of the increase in awareness and inclination of many people to ally their ethical principles with their investments and expenditure.

Ethical investments have outperformed the standard investments over the past 20 years and there is increasing interest in investing in ethical investment schemes. For businesses, the relevance of examining their products and services and identifying those with sound (or questionable) ethical standards will be relevant.

Buying goods direct from producers (through the fair trade schemes) rather than through large national or multinational companies, started in a small way several years ago. This has increased dramatically in the past few years and expansion should continue.

13.3.6 Building design

Buildings are likely to change in the next few years, with increasing efficiency of energy and other factors, including more sophisticated monitoring of internal conditions:

- Designing-in the capability for more individual control by staff working in the building is likely to be more typical in the next few years

- Designing-in space and systems for storing and collecting recyclate materials

- The buildings themselves will tend to be sited where there is better access to public transport

- The building materials will tend to be recycled and of a high specification. Heating and air conditioning systems will be more efficient.

The developers of buildings will also be expected to conform to higher standards of impact assessment, both in terms of the *construction* phase of the building and in the *use* phase.

13.3.7 Polluter pays

This is a clear principle set out by the European Union; in the UK it has begun to be enacted through the Landfill Tax and the Climate Change Levy. We can expect that further legislation will follow this pattern. Since such legislation is known well in advance, businesses should be able to prepare for it – so keeping a watching brief on the legislation, and keeping in touch with your business association, would be recommended.

The 'polluter pays' principle, if extended within the business, leads to a consideration of environmental economics, so that the financial impact of the business operations on the environment is carefully costed and actions can be taken to redress the problem.

13.3.8 Civil liability

Following trends in America, notably in connection with smoking and the tobacco industry, there is increasing concern about the extent to which businesses will be held legally responsible for the impact on the health of their customers and staff.

The fast-food industry is now being targeted for similar compensation, and with the general increase in litigation throughout the UK, businesses should be concerned with the extent to which their products or services affect, either directly or indirectly, their customers or the general public.

13.3.9 Risk management

Risk assessment is already a well-established, and legally required process as part of health and safety management; however, risk *management* and risk *assessment* are beginning to be used as techniques by larger companies and are likely to become more common.

Risk management as applied to environmental performance is already becoming well established and this will become more refined and more broadly applicable in the future. See – and use – the risk management form in Chapter 14.

13.3.10 Product durability

The 'buy, use and throwaway' society will definitely change over the next few years, as electronic and electrical goods are required to be re-engineered. This pattern may well be followed by other goods which are made to be more durable, easier to repair and to re-engineer.

13.3.11 Responsible tourism

Tourism is the largest industry worldwide, and can have a major impact on the environment, local society, the traditional economy and the whole national economy in some cases. 'Responsible tourism' is an approach which recognises that tourism is an important activity – but that it should take place in a way which minimises adverse environmental and social impacts.

13

13.3.12 Media

For most people and businesses, their perception of the environmental issues is dependent on information from the popular media. Invariably this is a double-edged sword, because it tends to exaggerate the problems and future difficulties – while simplifying the concepts.

This generally leads to a short-term concern, with a shallow understanding of the issues. It is unlikely that, in the UK, the approach of the media will change much; the environment will remain a passing concern when issues of a dramatic nature, or of concern to human health, arise.

13.3.13 Business start-up

In the UK, there is a steady and frequent turnover of businesses that start up and then take off – or struggle and fail.

For any process, it is much easier to start with the right approach and strategy rather than try to change matters at a later stage. Therefore, for any start-up business there is a tremendous opportunity to consider a whole range of environmental criteria and build these in to the business strategy from the start.

13.4 Summary

This chapter has not been an attempt to predict the future; rather, it has tried to indicate some of the changes which might occur over the next few years and which are indicated by current trends.

The essential message is that you should maintain good sources of information and should take steps to respond to the pressures which will, sooner or later, be affecting you, your business and your environment. Trade organisations and trade magazines are excellent sources, as are the various organisations listed on the next page.

13.5 Sources of information

Bioregional   Sustainable development approaches.
                                    www.bioregional.com

Centre for Environmental Initiatives
                                    London Borough of Sutton site, trying to find
                                    solutions to environmental problems.
                                    www.thecei.org.uk

ENDS   Environmental data services. Provision of
                                    general environmental intelligence. Useful
                                    in-depth magazine.
                                    www.ends.co.uk

Environment Business News
                                    Interesting articles.
                                    www.edie.net

Environment Times   Interesting articles.
                                    www.environmenttimes.co.uk

Envirosearch   Guide to the environment on the Internet.
                                    www.envirosearch.com

Envirotec   Technology focus.
                                    www.envirotec.com

Forum for the Future   Charity, whose mission is to accelerate the
                                    building of a sustainable way of life, taking a
                                    positive, solutions-oriented approach.
                                    www.forumforthefuture.org.uk

Green Futures   Business-supported organisation which
                                    examines new ideas.
                                    www.greenfutures.org.uk

The Guardian   The newspaper currently has significant
                                    environmental coverage each Saturday.

Sustainable Business   Best examples of how businesses use eco-
                                    efficiency.
                                    www.sustainablebusiness.com

World Business Council for Sustainable Development
                                    How big business goes about sustainability.
                                    www.wbcsd.ch

13

Appendix

Glossary of terms

Environmental risk assessment

Copies of forms

14

14.1 Glosssary of terms

BATNEEC   Best Available Technology Not Entailing Excessive Cost: a principle usually applied to technology investment decisions

BOD   Biological oxygen demand: a measure to indicate the level of pollution in water

BPEO   Best Practicable Environmental Option: a principle which can be applied in assessing investment or strategies

BRE   Building Research Establishment. www.bre.co.uk

BSI   British Standards Institute: information on management systems. www.bsi-global.com

CCL   Climate Change Levy: charge on all non-domestic fuel bills in attempt to reduce carbon dioxide production

CESMB   Centre for Environment and Safety Management for Business: specialist centre within Middlesex University offering support, training and advice to businesses. www.mdx.ac.uk/www/cesmb

CFC   Chlorofluorocarbon: major cause of ozone depletion – found in refrigerants, fire extinguishers and older air conditioning units

CHP   Combined heat and power: advanced and efficient boiler system which provides power and uses 'waste' heat within the system. Chapter 5

COD   Chemical oxygen demand: a measure of indicating level of pollution in water

EE   Environment Exchange: recycling packaging information. www.t2e.co.uk

EMS   Environmental management system

ETNA   Environmental training needs analysis: see Chapter 12

ETS   European Union Emissions Trading Scheme: see Chapter 5, p90.
www.defra.gov.uk/environment/climatechange/trading/eu/
www.environment-agency.gov.uk/business/444217/590750/590838/556574/?version=1&lang=_e

14

IPPC — Integrated Pollution Prevention and Control: legislation controlling particular processes

ISO — International Standards Organisation: information on management systems. www.iso.org

LCA — Life cycle analysis

nox — Shorthand term for nitrous oxide (NO)

PRN — Packaging Waste Recovery Note: certificate to demonstrate packaging recycling.

QMS — Quality management system

SEPA — Scottish Environmental Protection Agency. www.sepa.org.uk

sox — Shorthand term for sulphur dioxide (SO_2)

VOC — Volatile organic compounds: liquids, usually oil-based, which give off fumes – increasingly being recognised as causing health problems

WEEE Directive — Waste Electrical and Electronic Equipment Directive: recent legislation controlling the recycling of electrical and electronic goods

14.2 Environmental risk assessment

Every industrial process or business activity carries some sort of environmental risk, but assessing what may be 'significant' is an imprecise art.

For example, one environmental risk may be considered more significant than all others because it occurs (or is likely to occur) more often than others; another risk could be regarded as of great significance due to the likely effect on the environment – should it occur.   Assessing these risks considers a combination of the *likelihood* of their arising, and the *impact* of their occurrence.

There are two main considerations to take into account when conducting an environmental risk assessment:

- **Environmental aspect:** this is any element of an organisation's activities, products or services which interacts with the environment

- **Environmental impact:** is any change to the environment (whether adverse or beneficial) resulting from an organisation's activities, products or services.

14.2.1 Why carry out an ERA?

In general, all business or industrial activity affects the environment in terms of emissions to air, land and water.

More specifically, business activity causes, or is likely to cause:

- Depletion of natural resources

- Change in global climate

- An unclean and unhealthy environment.

ERAs are used in industry in the following areas:

- **Compliance with legislation**
- **Product safety**
- **Financial planning**
- **Site-specific decision making**
- **Evaluation of risk reduction measures.**

14

14.2.2 How to carry out an ERA

An ERA has the following basic elements:

- **Checklist:** know what you want to look at. Devise a checklist of all areas to tick off as you go along

- **Site survey:** watch what goes on. Consider what could go wrong – and how this could pose any threat to the environment

- **Staff discussions:** ask staff questions, especially as to how and why – and where – things go wrong

- **Documentation:** as well as an environmental risk, there is usually an associated legal risk to any incident.

14.2.3 Five steps to an ERA

Like any other risk assessment technique, an ERA will consist of the following stages:

Stage 1
Look at the hazards

Stage 2
Decide how the environment will be affected

Stage 3
Assess the significance of the risks

Stage 4
Record your findings

Stage 5
Review and revise where necessary.

Use the following model of an environmental risk assessment form to carry out an assessment in your premises using the above methodology.

Environmental risk assessment

Activity	Abnormal incident	Hazards	Likelihood*	Environmental significance	Mitigation
Filling drums with chemicals	Leakage during the process	Hazardous chemical mixing with ground water	3	Contamination of groundwater can cause diseases/illness	Drums to be filled in a contained area only

* **Likelihood:**   1=very low 2=low 3=medium 4=high 5=very high

14

14.3 Copies of forms

All of the forms and audits used and discussed within the book are reproduced here for convenience of reference. The forms should be used as a starting point – you need to consider the particular requirements of your organisation and your location – and the specific impact of legislation that affects you.

Of course, adequate space should be allocated on any form to allow for the capture of data, in a clear and unambiguous manner. All of the forms used here are necessarily condensed to fit the page.

The forms reproduced here are:

■ **Waste audit** (see Chapter 3 for in-depth information)

■ **Energy self-assessment audit** (Chapter 5)

■ **Energy tour audit** (Chapter 5)

■ **Principles of environmentally sound purchasing** (Chapter 8)

■ **Supplier assessment questionnaire** (Chapter 8)

■ **Environmental policy statement** (Chapter 10)

■ **Environmental review pro forma** (Chapter 10)

■ **Template to implement environmental management** (Chapter 11)

■ **Environmental training needs analysis** (Chapter 12)

Waste audit

Department	Paper *weekly qty* *used / wasted*		Cardboard *weekly qty* *used / wasted*		Metal *weekly qty* *used / wasted*		Plastic *weekly qty* *used / wasted*	
Office								
Storage								
Loading bay								
Waste skips								
Processing / Production								
Goods / Packaging								
Total waste per week								
x 52 = total waste per year								

14

Energy self-assessment audit

Week One

Day one:
Take a reading of the electricity or gas meter at the beginning of the first day of the week and note it below.

Day eight:
On the morning of the eighth day, take the reading on the electricity or gas meter and note that; the difference between the two readings is your energy consumption for a period of seven days.

> **Week One readings**
> Meter reading on day one   (a)   [   ]
> Meter reading after seven days   (b)   [   ]
> Energy consumption in Week One (b-a) [   ]

Week Two

Day eight:
Now start educating your employees with some good tips on energy reduction. Train them to follow these tips strictly from today.

During the week
Interact with the employees and see how they are performing. Remind them of these simple steps to reduce energy consumption. Print or buy posters of the guidelines shown earlier and post them on noticeboards in each department.

Week Three

Day fifteen
On the beginning of the first day of the third week, check your electricity or gas meter again and calculate the energy consumed during Week Two.

Day twenty-one
Check your electricity or gas meter once more, and calculate the energy consumed during Week Three.

> **Week Three readings**
> Meter reading on day fifteen   (a)   [   ]
> Meter reading after seven days   (b)   [   ]
> Energy consumption in Week Three (b-a) [   ]
>
> Units of energy consumed in Week One   [   ]
> Units of energy consumed in Week Three   [   ]
> Reduction in energy consumption   [   ]
> Money saved   [   ]

Energy tour audit

The audit over the next four pages indicates areas to look at, issues to consider and identifies possible actions needed. You need to complete a record of action taken – including, possibly, the timescale and the responsible person(s); you may also wish to include a note relating to the cost of the action taken, to allow you to compare this, subsequently, with the value of energy saved.

14

Energy use	Type of wastage	Action needed	Action taken
Lighting In offices lighting can account for about 50% of the energy consumption	• Inefficient lights • Staff not switching off lights when not needed • Over-lit areas, such as corridors and stores	• Use energy-saving bulbs and 26mm fluorescent tubes • Posters, advice, persuasion, encouragement, incentives • Switch off or remove some strips • Install movement sensors	
Heating The other major contributor to energy consumption in offices and factories	• Overheating – recommended temperature is 19°C • Identify areas where heating can be reduced • Draughts from doors and windows • Heating on for too long and radiators cannot be individually controlled	• Check the temperature independently (thermostats are not a very good indicator) and discuss with staff • Identify areas where heating can be reduced • Reduce temperature where possible • Fit door closers and draught-proofing seals • Check and vary timings month by month and fit individual thermostats on radiators	
Water Hot water is necessary but careless use costs lots of money	• Water is too hot • Taps are dripping • The amount of stored hot water exceeds requirements • Are all boilers and pipes well insulated?	• Reduce water temperature to 60°C but no lower • Repair and maintain • Check use level against amount stored. • Insulate as needed	

Buildings Effective insulation can save money and make staff more comfortable, but adequate ventilation is also needed	• Are heated and unheated areas effectively separated? • Are roof areas well insulated? • Are outside doors (and especially loading bay doors) open for minimum time? • Too much space to be heated?	• Check on heat flow from hot to cold areas. • Check and insulate • Check door mechanisms and fast-closing shutter doors • Consider installing suspended ceilings
Electrical equipment Electricity is expensive; simple controls on electrical equipment can make big savings	• Are computers, printers etc switched off when not in use? • Is air-conditioned computer equipment in the coolest area and properly cooled? • Do motors have variable speed drives (VSDs) fitted? • Equipment has poor efficiency rating	• Train staff and install automatic shutdown devices • Check and relocate and cool as little as necessary • Fit VSDs where appropriate • Select the most energy-efficient equipment when buying new
Boilers Poorly maintained boilers are a significant energy wastage	• Poorly maintained boilers • Boiler operates when not needed • Boiler is not the most efficient type • Boiler is too large for the requirements	• Check weekly, certainly monthly; service annually • Boiler *heating* turned off in summer, but hot water is still available • Consider installing a CHP system or a condensing boiler • Check boiler requirements

14

Compressed air Costs ten times more than electricity	• Leakage • Air produced is more than needed • Electrical equipment is an alternative • Air produced generally and not locally	• Check and repair • Provide only the minimum pressure required • Research the options • Locally produced air can be tailored to local requirements	
Vehicles Can make up to 25% of company energy costs	• Over-large company cars and vehicles • Poor driving practices • Poor maintenance • Petrol engine vehicles	• Offer staff small-engined vehicles • Driver training • Regular servicing • Investigate alternative fuels	
Buying energy Businesses often do not have the tariff best suited to their needs	• Not maximising on cheap-rate periods • Incorrect metering • Uncompetitive supplier • Not asking supplier to help you reduce energy consumption	• Check your tariff • Double check meter readings • Compare suppliers against tariffs and your use pattern • Some suppliers will provide expert help	
Other			

Principles of environmentally sound purchasing

Sample questionnaire

1. **Reduction**
   Reduction of the amount of material purchased – buy only the amount that is required.
   Can what you are looking to purchase be supplied in amounts that you require rather than in set amounts?   Yes ☐   No ☐   n/a ☐

2. **Reusability**
   Emphasise the purchase of equipment which can be reused.
   Can the purchase be reused?   Yes ☐   No ☐   n/a ☐

3. **Re-engineerability**
   Select, wherever practicable, re-engineered equipment.
   Is the equipment you're looking to purchase re-engineered?
   Yes ☐   No ☐   n/a ☐

4. **Recyclability**
   Can the purchase be recycled?   Yes ☐   No ☐   n/a ☐
   Is it easy to collect for recycling?   Yes ☐   No ☐   n/a ☐
   Is the purchase designed to be recycled?   Yes ☐   No ☐   n/a ☐
   Is the purchase itself recycled?   Yes ☐   No ☐   n/a ☐

5. **Sourcing**
   Research where the materials have been sourced from and investigate whether this is the best, or only, option, with regards to the environment.
   Have they come from a renewable (e.g. a forest) rather than a non-renewable (e.g. fossil fuel) resource?   Yes ☐   No ☐   n/a ☐
   Is that source certified as being managed sustainably?
   Yes ☐   No ☐   n/a ☐
   Can the purchase be viably sourced from a local supplier rather than be transported over large distances?   Yes ☐   No ☐   n/a ☐

6. **Type**
   Look at the composition of what you are looking to purchase; determine whether you could actually be purchasing a less environmentally harmful alternative in terms of the materials used.
   Have you researched into viable alternatives that might have a less environmentally harmful effect (e.g. NiH_2 batteries instead of NiCd)?
   Yes ☐   No ☐   n/a ☐
   Is the purchase free of toxic or hazardous materials?
   Yes ☐   No ☐   n/a ☐

14

7. Manufacture
Determine how the product (or products that a service uses) is manufactured.
Is the product (or product used as part of a service) consuming less energy in its production than alternatives (if any)?
Yes ☐   No ☐   n/a ☐
Is the product consuming less water in its production than alternatives (if any)?   Yes ☐   No ☐   n/a ☐

Is the product emitting fewer pollutants into the surrounding air/water/land during its production than alternatives (if any)?
Yes ☐   No ☐   n/a ☐

8. Use
Determine how the product's usage during its life span affects the environment.
Is the purchase more efficient during its use, in terms of energy, water and any other resources consumed, than alternatives (if any)?
Yes ☐   No ☐   n/a ☐
Are all health and safety issues regarding the purchase known?
Yes ☐   No ☐   n/a ☐

9. Durability
It is better to purchase products/materials that are robust and less likely to become obsolete in a short period of time.
Is the purchase durable?   Yes ☐   No ☐   n/a ☐
If necessary can the purchase be repaired?   Yes ☐   No ☐   n/a ☐
Is it easy to repair?   Yes ☐   No ☐   n/a ☐

10. Disposal
How the product or wastes produced during the fulfilment of a service are disposed of.
Can the product or wastes be segregated before disposal?
Yes ☐   No ☐   n/a ☐
Can the product or any wastes be recycled?   Yes ☐   No ☐   n/a ☐
Are there recognised less environmentally harmful ways of disposing of the product or any wastes?   Yes ☐   No ☐   n/a ☐
Are these alternative disposal routes cost-efficient?
Yes ☐   No ☐   n/a ☐

These principles, and how you have answered the questions above, will be used when determining the degree of environmental risk associated with your purchase.

Supplier assessment questionnaire

Section 1: Environmental management issues

1a Does your company have an Environmental Management System such as ISO 14001 or EMAS?
Yes ☐   No ☐   Don't know ☐

If 'don't know', please find out.

1b Does your company have an environmental policy or statement of principles, which details your approach to environmental issues?
Yes ☐   No ☐   Don't know ☐

If yes, please submit a copy of such policies.

1c Does your company have a person responsible for environmental issues?
Yes ☐   No ☐   Don't know ☐

If yes, please provide the name of relevant employees:

1d Has your company undergone an environmental audit?
Yes ☐   No ☐   Don't know ☐

If yes, please provide the date(s):

1e Have employees at all levels undergone training to aid understanding of environmental issues, impacts and policies within the company?
Yes ☐   No ☐   Don't know ☐

If yes, please provide the date(s):

1f Has your company been prosecuted in relation to any environmental legislation in the last three years?
Yes ☐   No ☐   Don't know ☐

If yes, please provide details:

14

Section 2: Operations approach

2a Does your company monitor and regulate the following areas within its operations?

Energy usage	Yes ❑	No ❑	Don't know ❑
Water usage	Yes ❑	No ❑	Don't know ❑
Solid waste	Yes ❑	No ❑	Don't know ❑

If **Yes** to any of above, please submit documentary evidence, such as two or three years' worth of meter readings or records.

If **No** to any of above, would you like information and assistance on how to monitor and regulate?   Yes ❑   No ❑

2b Can your company readily identify the following as a percentage of your annual turnover?

Energy consumption   _____   Water consumption   _____
Waste disposed of   _____   Raw materials   _____

If not, within what timescale can you make this data available?

2c Do you know what percentage of the raw materials used within your operations are virgin (i.e. not used before)?
Yes ❑   % = _____   No ❑

2d Does your company use any recyclable or reusable materials, and if not are there any processes in place to implement this?
            Yes ❑   No ❑   Don't know ❑

Section 3: Product/service delivered

3a Does the product or service that you provide contain or utilise any toxic or hazardous materials?   Yes ❑   No ❑   Don't know ❑

If **yes**, is there any risk of rogue emissions to air, land, or water during use and/or disposal?   Yes ❑   No ❑   Don't know ❑

Please submit documentation on any toxic or hazardous materials.

3b Has your company investigated the use of alternative materials, which are less environmentally harmful, in the provision of your product or service?
            Yes ❑   No ❑   Don't know ❑
If **yes**, have you implemented these materials?   Yes ❑   No ❑

3c Is your company aware of any legislation (environmental) that covers the manufacture or provision of your product or service?
            Yes ❑   No ❑
If **yes**, please submit a list of relevant legislation.

3d How does your company dispose of the waste generated during the manufacture or provision of your product or service? (Please give details of the different types of waste and how they are disposed.)

Environmental policy statement

Environmental Management System

Document No.:   Page: Revision No.:   Date issued:

Compiled by: Signed:

Authorised by: Signed:

Environmental Policy

Fisher Research Limited recognises that the pursuit of economic growth and a healthy environment must be closely linked.

Fisher Research Limited's Environmental Policy aims at integrating sound environmental practices into its operation. The policy has the following principles:

- *Regulations and Legislation:*

  To be fully aware of the requirements of all relevant current regulations and legislation and work with the appropriate authorities and organisations to achieve this, and to be aware of new and future legislation.

- *Waste:*

  To seek to minimise waste and promote waste recycling and the use of recycled materials, especially for packaging associated with the products it manufactures or supplies.

- *Energy and Resources:*

  To monitor the energy used in its operations and areas and install energy-saving practices.

  To take positive action on raw material and water consumption in order to preserve, as far as is practicable, natural resources.

- *Discharges and Emissions:*

  To reduce or eliminate as far as it is possible discharges and emissions to air, land and water, by improving processes, treatments and minimising risk.

- *Pollution Risk:*

  To take all the necessary actions to reduce pollution risk by:

  - improving all the areas where hazardous products are used or stored

14

- following strict procedures for storage and handling of hazardous products

- controlling and checking on a regular basis all processes and materials using or containing hazardous products

- devising emergency plans or procedures to deal with potential accidents or hazards.

- ***Products:***

   To continually review the environmental impacts of the products it manufactures or supplies and to work to reduce harmful impacts by research or developing new products.

- ***Suppliers and Customers:***

   To work as far as possible with suppliers and contractors to identify the best environmental practices and to high environmental standards.

   To strive to give customers the best available information to enable them to use their products in a healthy environmental condition.

- ***Organisation:***

   To integrate in the company's organisation an environmental structure, to ensure this policy will carry out, and follow through, environmental performances.

   To provide appropriate environmental training for all the company's staff.

   To ensure that all employees are aware that poor practices can result in hazards and risk to both the health and safety of employees and to the environment.

   To review and update this policy on a regular basis to ensure environmental issues arising from new developments are integrated in this policy.

   To conduct on a regular basis the audit and the review of the company's environmental performance to assess progress and identify any deficiency in order to correct it.

- ***Communication:***

   To communicate this policy to the staff, the suppliers, the customers and other persons that could be interested (e.g. insurance company, bank).

- ***Other aspects that Fisher Research Limited will instigate:***

   To seek to start an Environmental Management System.

   To prepare an annual report of the company's environmental and health and safety performance.

Reproduced by kind permission of Fisher Research Ltd

Environmental review pro forma

Organisation details

A: Organisation information

Company name   Contact name

Address   Tel
                                      Company size

B: Organisation's activity
Describe the company activity, including products/services, transport used, packaging used, recycling, re-engineering; also describe any prescribed processes. Indicate if the organisation is part of a larger group.

C: Management structure and organisation
For an effective implementation of environmental practices in an organisation, there needs to be someone with responsibility for environmental affairs; they should have clear levels of responsibility and be able to report to senior colleagues regarding decisions. It is also common practice to have a group of staff representing different departments in the organisation to contribute to environmental knowledge and developments.

■ Is there an organisational chart for the company?

■ Is there a member of senior staff with responsibility for environmental affairs in the organisation? If not, how are environmental affairs decided, documented and defined?

■ If there is a member of staff with responsibility for environmental issues, who do they report to, and where are decisions made?

■ Where are policies, documents and other information stored? How accessible are they for staff?

D: Policies
The policies published by an organisation are a reflection of its aims and aspirations and the extent to which it is trying to put identified strategies into place. Although a policy is a piece of paper, it will need to be demonstrated how it is being put into place, and how it is reported, reviewed and documented. The policies will also be a reflection of the main concerns and areas of operation of the organisation.

■ What policies does the organisation already have: Environmental? Health and Safety? Quality? Note any others that are relevant.

■ Are these policies published – and if so, where?

■ How are staff, the public and your customers made aware of your policies?

■ How are the policies implemented; who checks them?

14

Operational details

E: Product and process design

Adopting a cradle-to-grave approach to considering a product will include consideration of the design of the product. The process by which a product is manufactured is also important and should lead to consideration of how the process can be carried out in a more sustainable manner.

■ Can the design of the product be changed?

■ Are any products (or elements of products) subject to environmental legislation?

■ Can the product be made with less energy or water or by using recycled materials?

■ Can the packaging be redesigned and reduced?

■ What is the potential for repair, re-engineering or recycling of the product?

■ Are BPEO and BATNEEC principles applied to the product and its manufacturing process?

F: Materials, supplies and suppliers

The materials, resources and supplies that an organisation uses are an important aspect of the environmental impact. A tendency to identify and use recycled or re-engineered materials; to reuse materials; and to check on the environmental attitude and performance of suppliers is an indication of the environmental awareness of the organisation.

■ What raw materials are used, and what is the source of these materials?

■ What consideration is given to environmentally sound alternatives? How are these investigated and considered?

■ How is material use controlled? How are potential savings from resource efficiency identified, and are reverse logistics considered?

■ What controls can be exerted over suppliers? By whom and how (and when and how often) does this take place?

■ Are any hazardous materials used? Can these be substituted, by more environmentally sound materials?

■ What recycled or recovered materials could be used? Have these been investigated?

G: Storage

Legislation does exist for some materials but it is important that all materials should be properly stored, information about the materials documented, and a clear emergency procedure developed for use in the event of abnormal situations.

■ Is storage compliant with legislation?

■ List storage of hazardous materials, and any other items of concern, in the
   table below.

Material	Purpose	Controls	Location	Disposal

■ How often are stored materials checked? Are all materials properly
   labelled?

■ Are stored areas adequately bunded, and are bunds maintained?

■ Are storage areas reasonably secure?

■ What are the emergency procedures in the event of abnormal situations?

■ Any pressurised tanks?

H: Energy

*Consumption of energy is a major cost for many organisations, and also a
major opportunity for cost savings. The future trend is likely to be that energy
costs will rise as an attempt to control carbon emissions.*

■ What is energy used for?

■ What forms of energy are used?

■ What energy minimisation measures are used? What additional ones could
   be used?

■ How is energy use monitored?

■ What are the main areas of energy waste?

■ What is the potential for using combined heat/power boilers, solar power,
   landfill gas or other alternative forms of energy?

■ Are energy costs apportioned by section/department?

I: Water

*Water can be used in large quantities. For most firms their water supply is
metered so there is an incentive to control its use.*

■ What is water used for?

14

■ Where is water sourced?

■ What has been done to reduce water waste? What is the potential for this?

■ Is there potential to recycle or reuse water?

■ Are any materials discharged through the water?   Is there consent – and what about materials not consented? Fill in the table below.

Material discharged	From what process	Monitoring	Legislation

■ Is water discharge monitored – and are discharges to water monitored?

■ Are all pipes checked regularly for leaks?

■ Is any onsite treatment of water carried out?

■ What emergency power sources are available in the event of emergency?

■ What is the emergency plan if systems fail?

J: Emissions to atmosphere
The control of air quality is the responsibility of local authorities using strict legislation set out by the Government. It is an area of law which is being progressively tightened.

■ Are any materials (including dusts) emitted to air?

Pollutant source	Emission point	Abatement devices	Monitoring

■ How are emission levels reported, and how regularly?

■ Note any previous incidents of uncontrolled releases.

■ Describe plans for new abatement technology in relation to forthcoming technology.

■ What are the emergency plans in the event of an abnormal situation?

K: Waste

All organisations produce waste. The costs of waste disposal are increasing and are likely to continue to do so. The aim of any organisation moving towards sustainability is to reduce its resource use and minimise the wastes being disposed of.

■ Where are waste materials stored? Is their storage compatible with good housekeeping, good site operation and does it minimise risk of accidents?

■ Complete the table below.

Waste type	Waste source	Waste quantity	Principal component	Treatment

■ Are waste streams monitored? When, by whom, how often and how reported?

■ Are waste contractors used? Who, how often, what alternatives have been investigated?

■ Where is waste transfer documentation?

■ What alternatives to disposal might there be? What is the potential for recycling, or returning materials or equipment?

■ Is the organisation affected by packaging regulations?

■ Complete a waste reduction opportunities chart?

L: Transport

A key environmental area, and one likely to pose questions to every organisation.

■ What transport is used?   Specify what for, and approximate costs involved.

■ How are vehicles maintained?

■ What is the company's vehicle policy? Is public transport, cycling and shared car use encouraged? How?

■ What controls are placed on drivers of delivery/company vehicles, such as parking, speed limits?

M: Noise

■ Is noise an issue? What protection is available for staff, visitors, general public?
■ Have there been complaints?

14

N: Facilities management
Buildings all need looking after and this can have significant environmental impact.

■ Comment on heating, lighting, cleaning, furnishings, decorating, fittings, etc.

■ Also comment on external features, car park, landscaping and site management.

O: Site management
The way an organisation manages its site is important, both in the control of discharges and emissions from the site, and also in the overall appearance and the way that visitors view the organisation.

■ What is the history of the site?

■ What (and where) are the drains on the site? Where do they go – and are there any interceptors? Is there a readily accessible plan of the underground pipes, drainage and tanks on the site?

■ What are the storage facilities on the site? How susceptible are they to wind blow of waste?

■ Is the site near to any ecologically interesting sites, either land or water? How does the site impact on these or other areas?

■ What are the flood and emergency rainfall discharge measures?

■ Is there any evidence or risk of land contamination?

Management issues

P: Training
Training in environmental understanding, awareness and knowledge is necessary in order to spread the environmental strategy throughout the organisation. Training should also be a two-way process, encouraging and equipping staff to contribute to the environmental improvement process.

■ What environmental training is provided and to whom?

■ What environmental training is provided to staff in key positions (e.g. those who might have to deal with an emergency or abnormal condition)?

■ What environmental information is provided to new staff?

■ Is environmental performance included in appraisals?

- How environmentally aware and committed are staff? What are the indicators of this?

Q: Public relations
This includes how the company is seen by the public, how it tries to portray its green image, and what links it develops with local communities and how it affects neighbours.

- What environmental information does the company publish? Is this included with other materials or separate?

- What information is available to inquirers?

- How does the organisation deal with complaints? Are these logged?

- What contacts and relationships does the organisation have with local communities and neighbours? How far does this extend? What is the aim of these links and contacts?

R: Financial matters
This includes the investment, insurance and any purchasing policies that the organisation has. Current trends show significant interest in ethical investments.

- Are environmental issues considered when planning budgets and, if so, how? Who is making the decisions in this area?

- Is there consideration of environmental issues when investing in new equipment, sites or businesses? Is the purchase made only on the cheapest criteria or do environmental issues get considered?

- What environmental questions are raised when purchasing new equipment or materials?

- What is the organisation's insurance against environmental accidents?

- How are environmental savings identified in the finance controls – for example, is a cost/benefit analysis applied?

S: Marketing
- Are the products and services attractive to 'green' consumers?

- Are the sales staff aware of green consumer interest in products similar to yours?

- If the product or process were changed, would there be any market advantage?

14

Template to implement environmental management

ABC Ltd

1. Company structure

organisation chart

2. Management responsibilities

The implementation of our environmental policy at ABC Ltd is being followed in a considered and co-ordinated way.

…………….. (name) has overall management responsibility for the environmental policy throughout the company.

Environmental policy area   **Name/Position/Responsibility**

Legislation and compliance

Maintenance and emissions control

Waste and recycling control

Transport and discharges

All other environmental matters

Packaging

3. Environmental policy

Environmental Policy Statement

Doc No: Revised   Date:
                                 Authorised by:

At ABC we have a responsibility to the environment. Activities are regularly evaluated and environmental concerns are addressed with a view to selecting the best practicable environmental option.

The environmental policy has the following principles:

Regulations and legislation

Resources

Energy

Transport

Discharges and emissions

Packaging

Waste

Organisation

Communication

This policy will be made available to staff, suppliers, customers and any other person who might be interested.

Suppliers
We will work with our suppliers to ensure the highest quality of product is used and that information on types and strains of products are fully declared.

Signed: Position: Date:

4. Setting objectives

ABC Ltd recognises two types of objective:

- Improvement: moving forward
- Maintenance: keeping up a high standard of performance

A 'step-by-step' approach to setting up environmental objectives has been carried out:

1. Environmental aspects of policy have been considered
2. Environmental legal issues have been addressed
3. Priority issues have been set
4. Existing performance levels with regards to the important environmental aspects and legal drivers have been assessed
5. Improvement objectives as appropriate **AND/OR** maintenance objectives as appropriate have been established
6. The method of achieving the objectives has been set out.

14

Setting up objectives

Improvement objectives	Who	When	How
To reduce energy usage per tonne of product by 2% based on 2004 usage		End 2005	Energy-efficiency drives, lighting controls and optimisation of throughput
To provide environmental training for all staff where appropriate to environmental improvement		End 2005	Training packs, and coaching. Funding being sought
To reduce packaging		Ongoing	Reconfigure bags to use less material.
To improve drainage and discharge controls		Summer 2005	Initial mapping to identify issues
To lincrease range of resources, materials and equipment from recycled or environmentally sound sources		Ongoing	Continue to seek recycled alternatives to present materials
To increase range of materials recycled		Ongoing	Continue to segregate and monitor
To formulate and implement an environmentally sensitive purchasing regime		End of 2007	Decide performance criteria with suppliers; implement purchasing regime using tools such as periodic supplier reporting and audit
Integrated Pollution Prevention and Control compliance		March 2005	Work with CESMB to complete application.
Spill kit availability		January 2005	Purchase and include training

Maintenance objectives	**Method of achievement**
To maintain continual compliance with IPPC regulations	Compliance with existing factory operating procedures and criteria, maintenance of site cleanliness, efficient working and maintenance of filters and materials protection its instrumentation and hardware, constant monitoring, auditing or inspection
To adhere to sector guidelines	Regular checks on website, circulars and conferences
Maintain transport efficiency and considerations	Regular maintenance and selection of correct vehicle for correct load and journey
Continue segregating recyclate	Monitor performance and liaise with waste/recycling contractor
Monitor compliance with relevant legislation	Audit and check process and equipment on regular appropriate basis
Maintain awareness of new legislation and its implications	Visit Netregs site annually
Improve fuel monitoring	Monitor and record
Optimise load carrying and care in selection of new vehicles	Match load and vehicle and journey

Management of objectives

The objectives set out above and in future years will be discussed and agreed at the Senior Management meeting in January each year.
The agreed objectives and targets are then added to each department's aims and objectives.

14

5. Training

Staff training register

Name	Position	Training type/ Course	Course title	Date/duration	Course provider and location	Level of training*

*CPD Certificate and/or level of training

6. Reporting

Environmental reporting

Environmental objectives	Targets achieved 2004	Achievements/outcomes/benefits	Cost	Savings	Target for year 2005
examples					
Reduce energy use per tonne by 2%					
Environmental training					
Reduce packaging					
Improve drainage					
Increased use of recycled materials					
Increase recycling					
Environmental purchasing					
IPPC compliance					
Spill kits and training					

7. Additional Information

Suppliers

Supply chain: Environmental criteria in relation to supplier selection

ABC Ltd has introduced environmental criteria into the supplier selection process. Furthermore, we have developed an Environmental Purchasing Policy to ensure that goods and services purchased for the company are manufactured, delivered, used and managed at end-of-life in an environmentally responsible manner.

ABC Ltd now expects its suppliers to show evidence of their commitment to the environment by having an environmental policy.

Waste

The overall responsibility for waste collection and management within ABC Ltd lies with ....   (Director).

The current waste contractor for ABC Ltd is .... (company name); their Waste Licence number is ....

ABC Ltd does not produce any hazardous or special waste.

ABC Ltd will regularly scrutinise waste disposal and waste management processes to ensure that all controlled wastes are handled in a careful and environmentally appropriate manner.

Communications

ABC Ltd communicates openly about activities and prepares an annual report which addresses environmental policy performance and the achievement of policy objectives for the company.

Copies of ABC Ltd's annual report are available from Head Office to all our customers, employees and other stakeholders (partners, suppliers, contractors, and community group).

14

Environmental training needs analysis

Overall organisation needs

Organisation name:

Main activities (manufacturing/services and description):

Size/Number of employees:

How does the organisation currently impact on the environment?
For each topic in the table below describe how that impact occurs. If you
believe that the organisation has no impact on that feature of the environment
explain why? Some features have been included in the table and in the first
case an example is provided.

This should also include positive impacts on the environment so that where an
organisation undertakes work which enhances the environment this should be
noted.

Environmental feature	Type of impact	Cause of impact or reason for no impact	
Air	*Carbon dioxide*	*Burning oil, gas, for heating and lighting. Transport*	
Water			
Land			
Resources			
Waste			
Nuisance (noise, smells, visual)			
Habitats/wildlife			
Transport			
Site issues			
Indirect (via suppliers or customers)			
Other (state)			
Other (state)			

Does the organisation have an environmental policy?

What are the main features of the environmental policy?

What environmental legislation impacts upon the company – e.g. waste, emissions and discharges, packaging etc?

What do customers expect of the environmental performance of the organisation? i.e. has the organisation been asked about its environmental performance by any customers/clients?

What are the significant environmental costs of the organisation– e.g. is waste disposal significant, energy costs high? Costs of complying with discharge or emission limits?

How will environmental progress be monitored?

Considering these last three questions do your responses indicate the need for particular environmental training for staff?

What environmental training is currently offered by the organisation to its staff?

Has this environmental training been:
- One-off?
- Separate from other training?
- Linked to any other training?
- Repeated?
- Included in any induction training?

How can environmental training be integrated with the other training?

How are environmental messages communicated from the organisation to managers and staff? How continuous is this?

What other environmental communication techniques will be used to support the environmental training?

14